FAU: THE THIRD G

Front cover – An international work party unloading stone for hospital foundations, Ionian Islands, 1954   (PHOTO: JACK SKEEL)

Back cover – The first Section ready to embark for Greece, 1954
(PHOTO: JACK SKEEL)

FAU: The Third Generation

Friends Ambulance Unit Post-War
Service and International Service
1946-1959

Prepared and presented

by

Roger Bush

William Sessions Limited
York, England

ISBN 1 85072 211 0

Printed in 11 on 12½ point Plantin typeface
from Editor's Disk
by Sessions of York
The Ebor Press
York, England

Contents

Illustrations

Preface

THIS BOOK IS THE work of many hands. The response from former members of the FAU Post-War Service and International Service to the appeal from the FAU Committee for information, memories and memorabilia has made it possible. Without that response there would have been little to go on. Annual reports are necessarily brief documents, accounts and balance sheets still drier, and even the Unit's 'Occasional Information' news-sheets were – well – occasional.

So thanks are due to all those who sought out diaries, letters, photos, or who simply cast their minds back forty or fifty years and produced the scraps of material from which the quilt could be sewn together. The later years of the International Service, when its headquarters were at Lavender Farm, were already the subject of a compilation volume drawn up by the former General Secretary, which has been helpful in building a picture of that period. The earlier, Post-War Service, years have been similarly helped by the efforts of Richard Taylor, whose service spanned that time and whose contacts and judgement have given coherence to those chapters.

John Gray, a member of the FAU Council, contributed the note on the administrative background and much of the chapter on the formation of International Service. Sadly, though, there is something of a gap in the record concerning the foreign Associate members, young Germans and others who worked alongside British members both in this country and abroad. Serving, as they did, for shorter periods, in most cases their names were not retained on the general FAU Register, and many contacts have been lost over the years.

It was my judgement as editor that we had enough information from the various sources to construct a narrative history. There were offers of further material, as there were of editorial assistance, which it was impossible to take up if the job were to be kept within a scale and timetable acceptable to the FAU Committee and, through them, to members. At very least, though, this points the way towards the construction of an archive covering the thirteen years from 1946 to 1959, which can join those of the FAU's war years.

Factual accuracy is a problem when so much of the material has had to come from memories and recollections, but a certain amount of cross-checking has been possible. I have been helped by comments made at a gathering of former PWS and IS members in York in October 1997, and by members of the FAU Committee.

Especial thanks are due to the other members of the Editorial Sub-Committee: John Gray, whose letter to former members took us forward from the hopes and ambitions of the 1996 York reunion to a realisable goal, and Gerard Wakeman, so often the presiding genius at exhibitions of FAU memorabilia. And, finally, may I record my thanks to my son (Jim) for his help and guidance on processing, printing and copying to a father only just in touch with new technology; and to the Sessions Book Trust, whose financial assistance made the publication of this book possible.

ROGER BUSH
May 1998

Introduction:
The FAU in two world wars and after

"THE FRIENDS AMBULANCE Unit of the two world wars set out to be what its name suggests. Its story has been told elsewhere."

Thus opened the second annual report of the FAU Post-War Service in 1947. What was the history of this peace-time descendant of the FAU and of its successor, the FAU International Service? This brief account has been put together from the assembled memories of members of the two bodies and from the records held, like those of the war-time Units, at Friends' House in London.

The Friends Ambulance Unit was first established in 1914. It was a voluntary association of young men and women who organised themselves to relieve suffering caused by war. Although it was not an official agency of the Religious Society of Friends (Quakers), its members generally shared the Quaker attitude to peace and war and sought to follow the Quaker tradition of service.

Quakerism and pacifism have been linked since the seventeenth century. George Fox, widely regarded as the founder of Quakerism, was once offered a captaincy in the Commonwealth army fighting against the forces of Charles I. He declined it. In his diary for 1651, he writes: "I told them that I lived in the virtue of that life and power that takes away the occasion of all wars". The denial of "all outward wars and strife and fightings with outward weapons" became the Quaker "testimony to the whole world".

Not all young Quakers necessarily registered as conscientious objectors in either of the two World Wars or subsequently, nor was the FAU intake by any means confined to Quakers, but Quaker thinking was an unmistakable influence on the work, and on the organisation, of the FAU.

Prominent members of the Society of Friends were closely involved in the formation of the FAU in 1914, but from the very beginning there were arguments about its title and its activities. Some felt that it was bound to become part of the military system, others that its existence was fully justified by the inadequacy of any services devoted to acts of healing in the fields of conflict. Nor did the arguments cease after the early successes of the Unit in filling a gap and saving lives – of allies, enemies and civilians. In fact the introduction of conscription in 1916 brought matters to a head. A group who had already served within the Unit resigned on the grounds that military medical services were by then better organised and that, as conscientious objectors, they should not be regarded as accepting service that would help in the continuance of the war. As Corder Catchpool, one of the group, put it: "Men displaced from the services taken over by the Unit....were often drafted to the firing line and complained bitterly that I and my comrades had sent them there." Another complaint was that "the primary object of our work was the refitting of men to take their places again in the trenches".

It is not the purpose of this introduction to describe, even briefly, the work of the FAU in two world wars, but it is worth remembering those early conflicts of principle. In different ways they re-emerged in 1939 and even after 1946.

There are clear similarities between the men and women who made up the "Anglo-Belgian Field Ambulance Unit" in October 1914 and those who served in the FAU in World War II. And although the work of those who served in the FAU's Post-War Service and International Service was of a different nature, the same dilemmas about the right of the state to conscript for military service were in evidence right through until 1959, when the end of National Service had brought the activities of FAUIS to a close.

Of course more glamour attaches to the story of the war-time Units. But there is interest too in the peace-time organisations. These were staffed with much smaller numbers and with younger personnel; at no point did either Post-War Service or International Service have more than one hundred members, and a high proportion of these started their National Service soon after leaving school or college. What they shared with the earlier FAU was the wish to look for constructive work as a witness of their pacifism, whether it was based on Quaker attitudes, any other Christian ideal of service, or humanitarian reasons. The traditions of the FAU, including training camps, unpaid voluntary service in return for maintenance and a nominal pocket-money allowance, and a commitment to "go anywhere and do anything" (GADA), continued in the Post-War and International Service organisations. Indeed, the young people joining both benefited enormously from the input of older members of the FAU, as well as from the financial backing provided by Friends and others in the form of regular subscriptions.

The overseas work, at first mainly tied to the effects of war, came to include aid following natural disasters such as flooding in northern Europe and earthquakes in Greece. Always there was an emphasis on the need to bring understanding between young people by working on reconstruction projects especially concerned with young refugees or children whose social circumstances had suffered because of war or other disruptions.

A regimental history is usually based on accounts of campaigns. While the pages that follow set out in roughly chronological order the projects undertaken by the PWS and IS, there is a greater reliance on the experiences of individuals. This is appropriate enough, for those who joined the Units, while accepting a measure of corporate discipline, were often of an independent cast of mind, filled with ideals – some of them quite unrealistic – and of widely differing backgrounds and attitudes. This account arises from the stated wish of former members attending a reunion in York in 1996 that there should be some written record of these experiments in peace-time pacifism. The FAU Committee is grateful to all those who responded to the appeal for recollections, diaries, and any material illustrative of their time in the FAU.

CHAPTER 1

The FAU in war-time and the beginnings of FAU post-war service

DURING THE 1914-18 War the FAU worked in France and Belgium, on ambulance trains and motor ambulance convoys, and on hospital ships. It established its own hospitals for casualties in Dunkirk. It also undertook relief work in Belgium. Over a thousand served in it.

In 1938-9, when the storm clouds were again gathering over Europe, it was through the action of members of the old Unit that a new scheme to train volunteers for relief service and ambulance work was planned. Paul Cadbury was Chairman of the committee which took these plans forward. By the end of September 1939 nearly sixty recruits had joined a training camp at Manor Farm, near Birmingham, and the endeavour had again become the Friends Ambulance Unit.

But if those who planned the new FAU thought that it would repeat the pattern of activities of its predecessor, they had to adjust rapidly to a very different war. Mainland Europe was hardly in the picture, and an ambulance team sent to Finland and Norway had to retreat hurriedly, only just in front of invading German forces. It soon became clear that emergency relief work would be needed in Britain, following the bombing raids, and assistance was also needed in short-staffed hospitals. Meanwhile, the boundaries of the war were spreading. By 1945 the Unit was to see service in no fewer than twenty-five different countries in Europe, Africa and Asia.

In the Far East, FAU teams transported medical supplies along the Burma Road and undertook medical and civilian relief work in China. In India they were involved in Civil Defence preparations, as well as assistance to cyclone and famine victims. In Ethiopia and Syria the work was concerned with organising medical and health services. Later, following the Allied Forces through North Africa, into Sicily, Italy, Greece, Yugoslavia, the Dodecanese Islands, and then into France, Belgium, Holland and Germany, ambulance and relief teams found themselves working more closely with armies.

After the end of hostilities, FAU work was in course of being transferred to other agencies: in China the FAU China Convoy became the Friends Service Unit (China), jointly sponsored by the American Friends Service Committee and the Friends Service Council with headquarters in Shanghai. In Europe the Friends Relief Service and Friends Service Council took over work and some of the Unit members attached to it. But that was not quite the end of things.

At the declaration of peace in Europe in May 1945 it was to be expected that the Friends Ambulance Unit would be wound up, like other war-time organisations. And so it was, formally, on 30 June 1946, by which time the war in the Far East was also over. The Unit's members, nearly 800 of them in Spring 1946, returned to an interrupted education, to their former jobs, or continued their work by transferring to relief or welfare organisa-tions able to take over on the spot – mostly to UNRRA, Friends Relief Service and American Friends Service Committee.

But the post-war scene was full of uncertainties. The Council and General Purposes Committee, under its Chairman, Paul Cadbury, having decided on a closing date for the FAU, faced a number of problems which in the end pointed to the need for a successor body – FAU Post-War Service (PWS).

Firstly, conscription had not ended. As the closure date approached there were members working for the Unit who were not due to be released under the terms of their alternative national service. Nor was it known when the government would see fit to repeal the National Service Act. While there was no wish to appear to support peace-time conscription by letting the Unit continue to provide an alternative for conscientious objectors to national service in peace-time armed forces, something had to be done about the transitional period and to provide for young pacifists who would still be looking for a form of non-military service.

Straightaway it was recognised that PWS would be an independent, much smaller, and differently constituted body. For one thing its intake would largely be made up of younger people, typically eighteen-year olds. By 1947 its total strength was around 70, average age 19. Its work too would be different. Otherwise it would follow the pattern of its predecessor, its unpaid members receiving only maintenance and a nominal pocket-money allowance, though there would be a small core of older workers at headquarters who were paid a modest salary.

The effects of nearly six years of war presented plenty of opportunities for all sorts of relief work; it was a matter of fitting opportunity to the capabilities of such a small, young, body. How could PWS carry on the traditions of the FAU? The 1947 report sets out the underlying thinking of PWS at its most quixotic:

> "We do not drive ambulances nowadays; we rarely tie a bandage. But long ago in the days of the first world war our fathers learned (what the second war emphasised) that a casualty is not necessarily a wounded soldier on a stretcher. Even when he was, we often found that the really useful thing we could do for him was to bring him a mug of tea or a cigarette.
>
> We still help where we can with war casualties in the stricter sense. Of the jobs we have been asked to do this year, one has been to help the French Red Cross make a home for children who have lost limbs through bombs or mines.....
>
> As we have travelled Western Europe these past two years since the war we have acquired a mental background of grey, jagged, ruined walls, with holes through which the sky appears. They stretch from round the corner here in London, across France to Austria, Germany and beyond. In the summer we also noticed the same little pink flower which grows up out of the rubble in Holborn, went most of the way across

Europe too. In the endless procession of ruins we looked for the clumps of colour..... All over Europe there is a new life struggling to flower in the wreckage of the past. It is too early yet to say if it will succeed; in any case we have only helped to water a few random shoots."

The first PWS report, for 1946, summed up another aspect of the aims and intentions:

"Terrible as Europe's material needs are, the moral and spiritual damage resulting from the war is immense; and not least among young people. Our own members have escaped the worst of this damage, and because they are the contemporaries of young people who need help in Europe, they can work on an equal footing with those whom they try to help, expressing the friendship of another country in a service which the recipients can most easily accept. We do not dispense 'charity'; we offer labour, chiefly manual, supported by such resources as we can muster, to people who are struggling to help themselves."

Finance too was a problem. It became apparent that "relief" was going to be needed over a much longer period than had been foreseen. As the Friends Service Council told London Yearly Meeting of the Society of Friends in 1950: "...the shallow tilling of a wide field had revealed areas where deeper cultivation was required". Funds were scarce and by now there were several agencies competing for them. "Save Europe Now" was launched by Victor Gollancz; for a time PWS both assisted its efforts, by seconding staff to its London office, and received assistance from it. A longer-term relationship developed later with the Oxford Committee for Famine Relief (founded 1942). In 1949 "War on Want" – its name devised by Harold Wilson – broadened the terms of "relief" to include situations of poverty world-wide.

Little wonder then that the small-scale efforts of bodies like PWS, and even FSC, came under critical scrutiny, from within as well as without. "We make no claim for the virtue of 'service' as such. We do not press the virtues of such chimaerae as 'duty', 'self-sacrifice', 'self-denial', which we recognise are all too often signs of inward impoverishment."

That was the stern view taken by the FSC's 1948 Report, which also went on to observe that "the spectacle of a hundred or so workers seeking to meet the world's needs with less than a hundred thousand pounds" might seem "the very ecstasy of presumption". These were the years of post-war austerity, but it is worth remembering that a "Committee for Relieving the Distressed Inhabitants of Germany" once raised some £50,000 in little more than a year – and that was in 1806 when such a sum was worth perhaps half a million pounds in modern values. Even then, concerned voices still grumbled that it was not enough.

Somehow or other the resources were found. One of the first tasks undertaken by the Post-War Service in 1946 was to extend the work of an FAU team which had gone to Finnmark, northernmost province in Norway, where a scorched-earth policy had left hardly a house standing. As Tegla Davies noted at the end of his account of the FAU in World War Two: "Scandinavia was the scene of the Unit's first enterprise in 1940; it was the scene of its last in 1946. In Norway the new team was able to make use of a bank balance which had been hastily abandoned by its predecessor six years before".

CHAPTER 2

PWS – 'Constructive service for young Christian pacifists'

A FTER THE CLOSE-DOWN of the Friends Ambulance Unit at the end of June 1946, the first sole activity of the Post-War Service was to run its 1st Training Camp. This followed FAU tradition and was held at Manor Farm, Bristol Road, Birmingham, where almost all war-time FAU camps had been held. The camp opened to 28 new probationary members on 12 August. The five training officers were all experienced FAU men who brought a wealth of practical know-how for the benefit of the young pacifists. All but four of these were straight from their first job or from school sixth form. Somehow, self-discipline, corporate responsibility and practical skills had to be taught, accepted and absorbed by all.

The PWS Personnel Officer was Jack Eglon, who came as a qualified teacher with recent experience in German and Austrian schools. Two other officers had both been asked to extend their length of service to staff the camp: Len Parker as Training Officer, with Jesse Hillman, who had latterly been Quartermaster at the Gordon Square headquarters. Len Parker comments: "At twenty-eight, with over four years in the Unit and an overseas tour behind me, I felt like a veteran". Jesse Hillman writes: "As well as giving lectures, ensuring that we had food to feed the hungry and that it was well cooked, I also led route marches – and got them lost, acted as umpire on the 'Conchie Commando Course', and demonstrated how to construct outdoor cooking facilities in

9

the mud around Manor Farm". Two slightly younger officers, both with wide experience of trucks and driving, Deryck Moore and Brian Taylor, were the Driving Instructors. These five had the challenging task of training their young charges, in seven and a half weeks, to take the sort of positions of trust, responsibility and leadership that their experienced predecessors had taken. Since no-one could quite foresee the type of work PWS would undertake, the course followed the broad lines of FAU training – First Aid, driving and mechanics, cooking and nutrition, marches and physical training. Dr Rutter and Nurse Gibbs helped out with the first of these.

As for the trainees, one of them remembers: "Learning to drive a truck was great", but adds that "some activities – field cooking, for example – were hilariously inept and irrelevant. The first-aid element was not presented with any edge, and the St John Ambulance examinations were almost scandalously negligent (I passed)." Another comments that "Dr Rutter got his first principles across successfully", but a third felt the first-aid training was inadequate, and remembers "Dr Rutter recounting putting a patient in and out of a cold bath to reduce or restore body temperature" – a sort of first principle perhaps. However, it should be recorded that, by the time of the last Manor Farm training camp in 1947, Dr Rutter had given instruction to 1071 members of FAU and PWS at 22 training camps.

A somewhat unfair criticism of the camp was that it consisted almost entirely of ex-Quaker-school boys. Possibly 12 did come from such a sheltered, boarding school, background, and because of their service as school prefects, four were selected as Section Leaders. This mistake was not repeated in later camps. Most campers left with the Red Cross/St John certificate, and some with an FAU-PWS driving permit (members with the lowest grade were allowed to drive a vehicle in danger out of a burning garage).

Meanwhile there were two overseas projects already running. These were staffed by young FAU members who had several months of national service to complete and so, on 1 July, transferred to PWS.

Finnmark 1946: transport from Kvalsund was by fishing boat.
(PHOTO: RON ATKINSON)

The first of these projects was in Finnmark. Under the overall Section Leadership of Ron Atkinson, the twenty members were scattered in groups of two or three across this northernmost Norwegian province. When the occupying German army retreated in 1945 before the advance of the Russians they had left a disastrous waste land behind them. Norwegians had suffered much under the occupation, the northern livelihood was fishing, and the few remaining men had to gather food to store for the Arctic winter. Whole families lived in upturned boats and holes in the ground covered with peat. Swedish and American Friends saw it as a comparatively straightforward task for strong volunteers to build wooden homes supplied by Sweden, but there was first very hard manual work, hacking through the stony land to make foundations. It speaks well for the amateur builders that, when two of them, Peter Jackson and his wife Ulla (Glad), visited the site in 1993, they were able easily to identify their handiwork as weatherproof and still occupied homes.

Ron Atkinson writes: "We travelled overnight by train to Trondheim, and then slowly up the coast in one of the strangely named Express Route ships, crossing the Arctic Circle in the midnight sun and disembarking at Hammerfest, from where we went on by fishing boat to Kvalsund, which was to be the base of the Norwegian umbrella organisation, the Fredsvenners Hjelpetjeneste (Peace Friends Relief Service). There we helped to erect a 'barrack', after which most of us were sent off in two or threes, together with some of the Scandinavian volunteers, to work in outlying places. We, and indeed headquarters at Gordon Square, had assumed that we would stay together as a team. I think we would have been more effective that way, but the Fredsvenners were less task-orientated than the FAU and more concerned to promote international understanding by insisting on mixed-nationality working groups. In this respect their culture was closer to that of the IVSP than the FAU.

"Self-help in Finnmark was evidently the order of the day, and the evacuees (most of the population had been evacuated south) had returned and more or less housed themselves before we arrived, so that all that remained for most of us to do was to act as unskilled labourers for people building permanent houses. This was probably good for our souls, as well as our muscular development, and I was delighted to discover that I had learnt to discuss cement mixing in pidgin Norwegian for which I knew no English equivalent.....The enduring friend-ships we formed with the Norwegians and other volunteers satisfied, at any rate, the principal aim of the Fredsvenners." The FAU team withdrew in December 1946, though one or two stayed on into the New Year. Ron himself took ship under the Northern Lights at Hammerfest, travelled from Bergen to Newcastle with Peter Jackson, and arrived at King's Cross where he "had to cope with a distraught Lapp (due, I think, to appear on some television programme), whose two reindeer had become marooned in a van which had failed to reach the platform because of the length of the train".

The second project transferred from the FAU was in France. PWS was able to send a dozen men to help put up pre-fabricated buildings, again from Sweden, and extend accommodation at the College de Cévenol, Le Chambon-sur-Lignon, near Le Puy in

Haute-Loire. This was an educational project started by two pacifist pastors in an unusually Protestant district of France and, remarkably, kept going throughout the years of German occupation through the respect earned by their principles. It is claimed that they were even able to assist Jewish people out of the country. Co-educational and international, the college now had more than 300 pupils and a staff drawn from several countries. American friends bought the buildings, which were put up by the end of the autumn, and PWS helped the French and Americans and others with construction, with digging for roads and drains, and with the transport of material.

It had been the plan for the new entrants to PWS to go from their Training Camp to first postings in LCC hospitals, where all members were to work as brown-overalled ward orderlies and to absorb knowledge that a SRN was expected to take three years to learn, and that in a more controlled situation. As Peter Portwood points out, PWS was affected by the war-time experience that had got into the bloodstream of the organisation and its officers. "This was epitomised by the continuation of the London hospital placements. It would probably have been hard to justify that experience in rational and practical terms, but it was one of the most compelling and valuable slices of life that I had. I am glad the anomaly existed." Unlike the hospital work undertaken by the successor to PWS, FAU International Service, where wages earned were part of the justification, these were strictly placements, described in the 1946 Annual Report as "a period of ward work in London hospitals, useful for its general educational as well as its medical experience". Having to cope with bed baths, bed pans and similar humble tasks certainly prepared some for later involvement with any and every sort of domestic and medical work in France and elsewhere, especially where limbless children were concerned.

As things turned out, a temporary hitch with County Hall involved a stop-gap posting: all members were sent to report to Godstone Agricultural Camp. This too was a war-time relic. The "War-Ag" camps were where volunteers came to stay, paying for their keep and in turn being paid by farmers by the hour worked. Farmers would phone in their work requirements, and the volunteers were directed by harassed, clipboard-wielding clerks to the right trucks which serviced a massive area of Surrey and Kent. All right in theory, but on the first morning the truck arrived so late that some 10 PWS men, along with 20 or so volunteers, had to return to base, the farmer having refused all labour. Overall it is doubtful whether the PWS wages earned paid for members' keep and fares to Surrey.

However, within a week the hospital placements were sorted out and the young and inexperienced members were distributed to St Alphege's, St Charles's, St Stephen's and St Olave's – all Victorian LCC hospitals. The hospitals were very busy, six centre beds to each ward was not uncommon, the nightly casualty intake seemed endless, and the authority of Matron reigned supreme. So short of staff were the hospitals, and housed in buildings so vast and hard to administer, that even the raw PWS boys were made welcome and sometimes given work opportunities that untrained staff would never normally have. Those who went to St Charles's had the easiest acceptance, as a popular sister there had just married Len Parker, the Training Officer from the first PWS Camp. From that hospital, with its West End location, comes the comment of an elderly Cockney porter, who confided: "What comes through the Casualty doors in the evening is on the front page of the Daily Mirror in the morning". At St Stephen's, Fulham, Fred Deutsch remembers leaving a book on Freud in the Nurses Home sitting room and having it returned to him the next day in a plain envelope with a note from the Home Sister that he was not to leave it lying around as it would give nurses "ideas above their station". Diseases like tuberculosis were not uncommon in these hospitals. At St Olave's, Rotherhithe, Pat Alexander remembers swilling out the sputum mugs and staining slides for TB in the lab.

A second training camp was held in November 1946. Training of a different sort was also provided by two other home sections. Near Bridgnorth in Shropshire, two successive groups gave assistance to the Society of Brothers in repairing and refitting a large old farmhouse which was to provide a home for about thirty orphan children from DP camps in Europe.

And at Westhill College, Selly Oak, members helped to erect some pre-fabricated buildings, working under the supervision of professional builders. Apart from this, a group of members helped in the despatch of parcels by the "Save Europe Now" organisation after it became possible to send rationed foods and other articles to Germany in December 1946, and others took part as volunteers in medical research into pernicious anaemia.

The first purely PWS overseas work was at Vauréal. Following the Normandy landings in 1944, a Catholic orphanage near Caen was destroyed in the fighting. Children and staff set out on foot for Paris, where a Catholic priest, Father Pierre Levallois, persuaded the Government to requisition from the famous chocolate manufacturer, M. Menier (not a Quaker!), his broken and vandalised château and huge grounds near Pontoise in Seine-et-Oise. In October 1946 PWS supplied a team of workers and a truck, very useful in taking fallen timber from the grounds into Paris, where this valuable firewood was exchanged for equally valuable food for the orphans. There was a great amount of work to do on the estate itself, to restore the kitchen gardens and make the orphanage self-sufficient. Despite the limitations of school French in communicating with the staff and children, it was a happy centre, and geographically was a good position for the first footing by PWS on the Continent.

Germany looked to be a tougher prospect for the young PWS organisation, but by the close of 1946 a small party was sent out to join an international team, including Swedes, Germans, Danes and Swiss, working under the auspices of the Swedish Internationella Arbetslag and Swedish Red Cross, putting up pre-fabricated huts at Hamburg to form a social centre. This aimed to give practical as well as social help; a simplified method of shoe-repairing was taught and sewing facilities were provided, as well as a kindergarten and youth club.

By the time the second (1947) Annual Report of PWS was published it was able to report that "all our present workers have now been overseas, and foreign service has been a main objective, not only because of needs abroad, but because we consider that first-hand experience of foreign work can bring the beginnings of an understanding of what is really involved in peacemaking".

CHAPTER 3

From the Arctic Circle to Africa

IF FOREIGN SERVICE was a main objective, Post-War
Service certainly succeeded, during 1947 and early 1948, in
maintaining a good proportion of overseas sections, and that on
an income based largely on subscriptions and donations.

Post-War Service took over the lease of the old FAU headquarters at 4 Gordon Square, Bloomsbury, together with the
cellar of No. 3 as a store, on 1 July 1946. The building had to
serve as administrative centre, a hostel for staff and members in
transit between sections, an office and stockroom. The half-base-
ment contained the kitchen and dining room.

In forming PWS, the FAU Council had searched for and
employed two ex-FAU men – Jack Eglon, a teacher with years of
FAU experience in Germany and Austria, as Personnel Officer,
and Ian Robinson, who had spent most of his FAU service in
Ethiopia, as General Secretary. Together they formed an excellent team, and most of the successful day-to-day working of PWS
must be credited to them. The one secretary/typist, Dorothy
Stapleton, was also an ex-FAU member. The rest of the work at
headquarters was shared among the young, mostly 18-year-old,
members. They found themselves suddenly given titles and
responsibilities: two Catering Officers, a Finance Officer,
Assistant Finance Officer, Quartermaster, Assistant Quartermaster
and Movement Officer. A pushy salesman for Ofrex who called at
the office remarked: "What a lot of office boys; where are the
staff?". But the office boys rose to their responsibilities – hot food
was provided, donations acknowledged, bills paid, uniforms and

16

equipment bought, stationery ordered and travel tickets purchased. George Spencer, with accountancy skills, who had stayed
on from his FAU service to see the office set up, resigned from
PWS to follow his career, but his place was taken by an
Australian Friend, Ernest Roberts, a qualified accountant. The
bulk of Head Office staff, though, were on short-term placement,
and after three or four months usually joined a team at home or
abroad. Jack Eglon was always keen to see that there was no rift
between Head Office and field staff. In 1947 he took over as
General Secretary when Ian Robinson left to join a London
Missionary Society training college. John Swindale, again
ex-FAU, came in as Administrative Secretary and transferred
eventually to International Service at Petersfield.

The first year of PWS had started with a team up in the
Arctic Circle; the second saw a section, under the same Section
Leader, Ron Atkinson, posted to Equatorial Africa.

A five-man team assisted in a nutritional survey carried out
by local authorities in the Serenje district of Northern Rhodesia,
some 250 miles north-east of Lusaka, in what is now Zambia.
After a crash course on nutrition at the London School of

*Northern Rhodesia, 1947: treating a
youngster's leg ulcer – not part of a
normal day's work on the
nutrition survey.*
(PHOTO: RON ATKINSON)

Tropical Medicine, handily around the corner from Headquarters, they sailed out to Africa to work in the bush in a district divided into eight chieftaincies of the Lala tribe. These people lived in small villages of 12-15 households in wattle-and-daub huts.

Ron Atkinson writes: "Our principal job was to act as data collectors for the Nutrition Officer. The routine that was in due course established involved our spending a week at a time in each of three widely separated areas, and every fourth week at our base in Kalwa farm. This was the property of the Moffatt family, early missionaries in the area – in fact the grave of Livingstone himself was not far away. In each of the outlying areas we had a mini mud and thatch village built for ourselves, from which we went out and tried, using a prepared checklist, to get details of food supply and consumption in a group of African villages over a whole twelve months. Occasional visits were made to other villages for the sake of comparison. The local language was hard, though some of us did better than others. Mostly we had to cross-question villagers (usually women, since the men were often away in the copper mines) through interpreters, whose accuracy we in time learned enough to assess. The presence of an interpreter, a familiar figure then in the African scene, probably increased the seriousness with which our questions were treated, though irreverence not infrequently broke through. Verification of the responses was inevitably a problem, but comparing answers received on successive visits was some sort of a check. On the whole I believe that our data were good enough to enable the Nutrition Officer to present a reasonably accurate picture in her ultimate report."

"We were encouraged too, rather against our better judgement, to take on the uphill task of assessing the food intake of infants, who were normally breast fed for two or three years. Since demand feeding was the rule, it was difficult to distinguish times that were before or after feeds. Indeed, it was extremely difficult to weigh children at all. Few mothers would release their offspring as they sat unsteadily on our scales. Fortunately our efforts were perceived as amusing and were quite popular with the villagers."

"More pointful were our efforts to calculate crop yields.... The local agricultural system was a version of 'slash and burn'. Men, often returning from the Copper Belt for the purpose, would cut down large areas of trees and burn them in a series of small bonfires, so that finger millet could be planted in the ashes, with perhaps cucumbers and gourds in succeeding years. (The duty of cutting a separate lot of trees for each wife was said to be an obstacle to polygamy, which was not very common.) We measured the burnt areas and paid villagers to reap the millet, which we duly weighed. The system was sustainable only for the sparsest population.... the Agricultural Department was trying to encourage the adoption of a less destructive system."

"We must have missed some opportunities and made some mistakes, but all in all we were quite well matched to the specific task assigned to us and, I think, made a positive contribution, as well as gaining an eye-opening experience of rural Africa in the last days of colonialism."

Back at home, PWS sought to follow the tradition evolved overseas, though most of the work done by sections in this country was the giving of temporary service to meet special needs. Thus for some weeks members lent a hand in the small one-man hill farms of the Black Mountains, near Abergavenny, where winter gales had done a lot of damage. Others went in small groups to assist in repairs, cleaning and painting and work in the grounds of Salvation Army centres and rest homes.

A link with the wider problems of Europe came through PWS assistance to "Save Europe Now". This was a scheme devised by Victor Gollancz in 1946, under which people in this country wrote in with the name of the occupation zone of German friends and sent a 4s. postal order and stamped addressed envelope. They were sent in return a parcel label in the appropriate zone colour. The response to this, the first chance to send food and clothing direct to Germany, was overwhelming, and soon sacks of mail filled the office at Henrietta Street, Covent Garden. PWS members were drafted in to keep down this mail mountain and to help with the bottleneck of letters unsure of the correct zone. In an inner room was a map covering a whole wall and divided into

Russian, French, American and British zones. Opening the mail, checking the zones, postal orders and return envelopes with the right labels, was an incredibly boring task, but there was satisfaction in helping with this new initiative. Later, in 1948, the organisation had a depot at Parliament Hill Fields, and members assisted there as storehands. According to Ian Robins, clothing for Europe was also packed in the basement of Foyles bookshop in Charing Cross Road. "Our sorrow was", writes one member, "that well-meaning people had sent totally unsuitable goods such as dainty, fashionable high-heeled shoes or lace stockings when what was wanted was sturdy, warm wear".

Meanwhile, in France, the work at Vauréal proved a springboard for a succession of participatory assignments attached to various French ventures designed to give aid to young people.

At another semi-derelict château, this time at Longeuil-Annel, PWS co-operated with Don Suisse, the national relief organisation of Switzerland, in supporting the foundation of a farm and colony where difficult and maladjusted boys could be taught a variety of trades. Manual labour, driving, digging, and glazing windows in walls which still bore the marks of the First World War, were the main contribution of the PWS team, but during their five months there they also assisted in providing sports and leisure activities for the boys.

Not far from Vauréal there was further work with war orphans at the Château de Grouchy, Osny, from April 1947 until the end of October 1948. Here the work was concerned with helping the orphanage get on its feet, by bringing the vegetable garden into production, restoring paths and tidying the grounds after successive German and American occupation of the twentieth-century château, and later by providing transport. Peter Jackson and Mark Chamberlain took one of the invaluable Bedford trucks out to France in March 1948, and Peter, with Mike Abbatt, formed a two-man team to get the maximum use out of it. Though many of the children at Osny were orphans, organised under four "group mothers", others, writes John Pellow "had parents who were in gaol for alleged collaboration with the Germans. In fact, one of the girls who worked in the kitchen had had her head shaved for that reason." Living quarters for the section were in an old building that also housed an ancient generator worked by a water wheel. A balcony overlooked the railway line to Dieppe; "anyone who knew would wave a towel out of the window of the boat train as it passed by and some supper could be saved for them". At Osny there were opportunities to mix with the local village community: "Ian Robins became the projectionist at the local cinema. A band was formed – Les Cinq Cloches – which played at village dances in the area. Dennis Binns was on drums, Andrew Rogers played the piano, Ian Robins the accordion, Pat Alexander the guitar, whilst Ray Effemey was the vocalist."

In June 1948, Jack Eglon and Alan Bowness paid a visit to the French sections then working – Osny, Les Mesnuls and Boulleret – and met again French friends who had facilitated PWS work. Madame la Baronne Mallet was the guiding spirit behind Les Mesnuls and Boulleret. The first was a grand château near Rambouillet "given to the French Red Cross as a base for the rehabilitation of children badly wounded during the Liberation" writes Giles Heron, one of those who served there.

"As with other sections, the purpose of our original project was to restore both grounds and buildings to productive and habitable conditions by months of the familiar humdrum chores – scrubbing and repainting, weeding and digging, sawing wood and endless potato-bashing. But I fancy we at Les Mesnuls had the most interesting and rewarding time because we found there was so much we could do to help the children, and before the restoration was complete we were asked to stay on. We had created a niche for ourselves, not just by the simple, physical assistance we could offer – cutting the meat on the plates of the one-handed, playing football with the one-legged, even climbing trees with the no-legged! – but by our companionship and emotional stability. We raised funds from friends at home which enabled us to buy a small Christmas present for each child and to equip modest hobby clubs which we ran in the evenings, aero-modelling, painting and stamp collecting. Our social life contrasted starkly with work time. In appreciation of our voluntary service we were invited into comfortable and artistic homes, to a barbecue and a wedding reception, to swim in a private pool and to play on a private tennis court, to stay overnight in Paris apartments after enjoying opera and theatre." Peter Portwood too remembers: "We were royally entertained by local people who were seriously rich and had charming – and, in some notable instances, 'beautiful' – 'children' of our age; at which age it was a heady experience. The rather Spartan regime of the Red Cross children's home was a healthy balancing factor."

At Boulleret, which is near Cosne, in the middle of France, Madame Mallet had asked for help in restoring buildings that were to form a "preventorium" – a home to which youngsters in danger of TB could be sent for good food and living conditions. As the 1947 Annual Report noted: "Our work is acceptable because we are considered reliable, and because we give our labour. In France, unlike Germany, we are given our food in return. All our teams are equipped to be as self-supporting as possible, and we supply many of the necessary tools."

At the time of Jack's and Alan's visit the work in France was beginning to come to a close in anticipation of the end of PWS. But mention should be made of the other French sections: at Belval in the Vosges where a smaller, more modern, château of grey granite, damaged by occupation and by a delayed-action bomb, was turned into a children's colony for youngsters from the Strasbourg area; at Montmartin-sur-Mer, near Coutances, where a pre-war holiday camp for poor children from Paris was restored to its former use; and the two-man team that worked alongside German prisoners of war to repair the pillaged Château de Pomeyrol at St Étienne du Grès, in Provence, to form yet another of the "maisons d'enfants".

In Germany the infrastructure was very different, and it took longer to get sections established, but the initial work camp experience at Hamburg led to two members undertaking similar work at Hildesheim, near Hanover. And in the British sector of Berlin there was an opportunity for three members to take part in the activities of a Jugendhaus set up by Salvation Army, FRS and IVSP relief workers. This was a link with the war-time FAU, which in 1945-46 had been in charge of organising camps for a group of young Berliners evacuated to Austria, returning them to Berlin when conditions permitted.

A larger section, of six members, was sent in October 1947 to help the German Evangelical Church in a project to turn former German naval barracks into a hospital and old people's home. This was at Farge, in the sandy dune country outside Bremen and just inside the British zone.

Elsewhere in Northern Europe, PWS members took part in work camps in Belgium and the Netherlands. At Boussu Bois, a mining village near Mons, an IVSP camp was engaged in making a children's playground for a war-destroyed school – "rehabilitating an old slag-heap", as Fred Deutsch, one of three who went there, describes it. The whole camp went to Brussels for the celebration of the anniversary of VJ Day, and celebrated so well that he and one of the other volunteers missed the last train home and had to ask the police to accommodate them: "I clearly recollect being locked into a cell whilst their radio played 'Don't fence me in'". With John McCann, Fred was also at Gennep, near Venlo, in the Netherlands – "must be one of the smallest work camps in the history of SCI", he writes, "Just six of us doing unskilled rehabilitation work, mainly in the gardens of a TB sanatorium that had been vandalised by occupying and liberating forces."

Similarly small numbers helped in Austria, at Brixlegg, near Innsbruck, helping AFSC rebuild houses destroyed during the war and going on to join American and Danish relief workers in Vienna. Here more members joined them to work on clearing rubble from a damaged children's hospital in the Russian sector, after some weeks at a less than successful attempt to involve Austrian students in a joint work camp based on farms in Farrach, in Carinthia (see Chapter 10).

CHAPTER 4

The beginnings of International Service

A S POST-WAR Europe emerged from the bitterly cold winter of 1947-48, it became clear that it would soon be less easy to find opportunities for work that PWS could handle well. The real post-war emergency was over. New needs and new opportunities there were, but they would call for a new approach.

If PWS did not change, it would die. It was threatened both by a lack of suitable relief work abroad and by the prospect of a lack of life-sustaining donations.

The overall need for reconciliation in Europe, rather than just its physical reconstruction, began to preoccupy Jack Eglon. At heart a teacher and an idealist, he felt deeply about the many young people among whom he had worked for over three years both in Britain and continental Europe. Should PWS close down and a new vehicle be constructed that would marry up the idealism of young pacifist conscientious objectors and the new needs of European young people? In this way Jack Eglon became the architect of a plan for a "New Service", later to be called the FAU International Service.

Although Jack would have placed the creation of international understanding high among the objectives of the new organisation, it is quite possible that the origin of the name was a PWS poster and handbill which promoted the idea of (Inter)National Service.

To strengthen his own position in the Spring of 1948, Jack first sought two commitments from about twelve carefully selected PWS members. First, he wanted an assurance that each would assist him in the planning of the new service. Second, he needed a promise that each would extend his period of service beyond his normal date of demobilisation. For some this meant a year's deferral of entry to university. For all it meant a delay in entering properly remunerated employment. But nearly everyone accepted the invitation, proudly and gladly.

Fortified by this support, Jack travelled and consulted widely. He needed the understanding and co-operation of Quaker schools headmasters, for example, since their senior pupils were likely to form a sizeable proportion of forth-coming intakes of members. He wanted the Society of Friends to understand the novelty and the magnitude of the scheme that was taking shape in his mind. Most of all, he needed the backing of the FAU Council.

The younger PWS members who had accepted his invitation to become "a closely knit group of experienced people willing to shoulder the corporate burden of the new establishment", he led in a ten-day retreat to a borrowed cottage at Kingsbridge in South Devon. From this period of debate and critical study, the group emerged with its convictions firm and clear.

In due course the FAU Council agreed that the proposals for an International Service were valid, and that they could legitimately be realised within the terms of the FAU Trust Deed. It should be remembered that the Council included many war-time FAU members who were understandably keen to guard the reputation of the Unit as an organisation that had two simple functions: providing a vehicle by which COs could serve their fellow men, and relieving the suffering caused by war. It was not, on the face of it, obvious that Jack Eglon's proposals needed to be – or could or should be – fostered by the FAU. Should the FAU's war-time tradition and reputation be hitched to the more radical aspects of International Service? Generosity prevailed and agreement was reached. From that point FAUIS never lacked the support of the body of distinguished, busy, men and women who served on the Council and its General Purposes Committee (see Appendix 2).

Just how radical these proposals were may be judged from the following extracts taken from a lengthy document issued in mid-1948 and headed "A New Experiment".

"Against the enormous needs of the times there is very little we can do. But that is not a valid reason for doing nothing. A small experimental beginning has often led to larger developments in social progress, and some of us feel drawn to consolidating the experience and methods of FAU and FAU PWS in the project explained below. The scheme recognises a) that any such work must be practical and useful, b) that it will not be able to depend on many older full-time leaders for training young workers and administering the work, and c) that it will have implications of considerable educational importance.

It is planned to establish first a permanent headquarters settlement in the country in England, where young Englishmen and young Germans (with other nationalities, possibly, later on if the initial work succeeds) can live together, work on neighbouring farms, and follow a broadly educational and social course in an international setting. The farm work is an attempt to meet some small part of the country's needs in agriculture. The educational work will be linked with a neighbouring university.

In order for our scheme to function efficiently it must be realistically founded. We have therefore planned that our new headquarters shall be in a camp large enough to accommodate all our members, and from which all our activities can be co-ordinated. (Our present small London headquarters at Gordon Square will be vacated on 31 December 1948.)

But this foundation itself cannot be made until we have trained new entrants to the service, for our work requires careful methods as well as the right spirit. Hence our proposed programme is as follows:

1. A training camp at Manor Farm, Northfield, near Birmingham, lasting approximately 2 months and beginning on Wednesday 4 August 1948.
2. The establishment of the headquarters camp and its agricultural work. This involves lengthy official negotiations, which have already been in progress for some time. It is hoped that a camp in Yorkshire will be made available to us in the Autumn of 1948. (The date of our taking over the camp will determine the length of the training camp at Manor Farm, which may have to be extended for several weeks.)
3. The reception of a small group of selected young Germans, about 6-10 at first, who will join us either at Manor Farm or later at the headquarters camp....
4. The establishment eventually of further foreign work. As this memorandum is being written there is a possibility that we continue certain work in France from present PWS commitments, without a break.... We hope to have further work in Germany later on, but it is too early to give details of this, and much will depend upon the abilities of the new entrants in August 1948."

The training camp, it will be noted, was to use the accommodation previously used for the same purpose by the war-time FAU, and by PWS. New members were to be divided into groups under the leadership of experienced members of the Service. The routine arrangements included an obligatory morning run around the lake, a rest-hour following lunch, and a rigidly enforced lights-out. The statement of Training Aims gives a good idea of the ambitions of the project as a whole:

"From more than eight years of full-time international service by young people we have certain practical experience which must be handed on to all new entrants. Hence our training course. If twenty people come together for training they will probably have twenty different pre-conceived notions as to what that training should be, and what our work is. Obviously they cannot all be right, and in fact usually none of them is!

The main aims of the training camp are therefore:

1. To share ideas about the realisation of our ideals of a youth service devoted to international reconstruction and reconciliation. To learn more about the implications of those ideals, and to modify our personal conceptions in the light of the corporate life of the service.

2. To get to know each other well as comrades.....at work and leisure. To create a friendly understanding on which to build the international development of our work later on.

3. To get plenty of exercise to train ourselves physically for the work of the service.

4. To acquire a smattering of certain practical skills ...(it can only be a smattering in the short time available).... Any course we might choose would have serious limitations; the one actually chosen has been worked out in the light of many practical considerations as well as ideal conceptions..."

and concludes: "But there is a danger, too, in supposing that we can put our purposes easily into words; the spirit of the camp speaks rather for itself".

John Gray was one of those who promised Jack Eglon that they would extend their service to set up a new headquarters and organise training. He writes: "At one time I explored in depth the possibility of occupying Ganton, an ex-POW agricultural workers camp on the northern slopes of the Yorkshire Wolds overlooking the Vale of Pickering. There was also the possibility of establishing an HQ and Base Camp at a similar camp at Trumpington, near Cambridge. Eventually we chose Petersfield, after advertising in The Friend and getting a helpful and generous response from the Bursar of Bedales School."

And it was The Friend that carried an article, "Goodbye Gordon Square and Hail Petersfield", on 29 October 1948. "A group of experienced Post-War Service members is now extending its service to help launch the new venture of FAU International Service. We are not primarily an alternative to military service for young conscientious objectors. We have particular aims, and while it is conscription which brings most of our members to the point of deciding to join us, such work as we have in

prospect ought to continue even if conscription ended tomorrow..... For us it is a Christian duty to break down the walls of
ignorance and prejudice which still divide the countries of the
world. We would like to see our small beginning grow into a
broader effort which could include more young people than the
few who are as yet able to join us."

The new HQ, with its storage areas, garage and domestic
accommodation was always intended to house more than just
HQ administrative staff. Dunannie was a large Victorian house
with two and a half acres of grounds including a neglected
kitchen garden. It was adjacent to Bedales School at Steep, some
three miles north-east of Petersfield. Placed in charge of the physical arrangements, John Gray comments: "A good library, for
example, was considered desirable to permit visiting foreign
associate members to learn about Britain. Petersfield was a less
ambitious (and less austere) undertaking than either
Trumpington or Ganton would have been. Jack Eglon saw the
necessity of furnishing Dunannie as an attractive and decent
home for visitors of all sorts – a very particular sort of Quaker
international centre."

The move from Gordon Square, the closure of PWS and the
start of International Service happened quietly in the autumn of
1948. A working party drove down there in HGH 68, one of the
trusty Bedford trucks that were so much a part of the life of the
Unit, with a full load of office and domestic equipment. John
Gray, Peter Jackson and Richard Taylor were three PWS members transferring to the new service. Richard remembers drawing
the short straw and trying to produce breakfast toast on a cold
and un-cooperative Aga without the necessary double racquet. A
personal call at the local Ministry of Food office to register was
followed by a clerical mishap when the Unit was mistakenly
recorded as "The Thames Ammunition Unit".

Gordon Square was finally vacated on 22 October, and by the
following month there were 23 members at Dunannie. Many
were engaged on reconstruction work in the house and on restoring the grounds. The Hants and Sussex News sent a reporter to
investigate the newcomers. His report, headed "Dunannie House

may be centre of Peace", quoted Jack Eglon: "We are trying to do a kind of social first-aid, and we think that practical experience should be the basis of our religious and idealistic approach to the problems of internationalism. We want young people to learn, not just intellectually, what is involved in the building of world peace. We want to give to the potential young peace-builders an experience just as effective for their purposes as military training is for the fighting man."

As for the first recruits to the International Service, they were able to go to the new Petersfield HQ following an extended training camp at Manor Farm. At Dunannie they found a nucleus of ex-PWS members with Jack Eglon as General Secretary and John Swindale as Administrative Secretary. A fuller description of life at Petersfield is given in the next chapter. The HQ community consisted of an administrative and housekeeping team and a work pool that supplied labour to a number of local farms and earned vital supplementary income. The belief that learning something of the life of the agricultural worker was important in promoting understanding among nations and peoples may seem a little strange nowadays. But in the 1940s there was a great deal of interest in figures like Gandhi and their ideas of agrarian reform. Moreover this was at a time when far more people were employed on the land, when war-time food shortages were still fresh in the memory, and when some goods were still rationed. In Europe there were even worse shortages, and farming operations everywhere had suffered from a lack of labour. Certainly, farmers in the Petersfield area kept the work pool fully occupied after a slow start in the early wintry months of 1949.

As the Associate Members from overseas arrived, the value of the community's social life was enhanced. A full programme of recreational and leisure activities, film shows, talks, visits and discussions helped towards the educational aims of International Service which had figured so largely in its planning. Though the number of young Germans at Petersfield dropped towards the end of 1949 (changes in the documentation arrangements and the status of the Deutschmark were partly responsible), they built up again during 1950, several members arriving in time to take part in an International Weekend in April. Invitations had been sent to young people from fourteen different countries, and the non-Europeans included representatives from Africa, China, Ceylon and America. Gerald Gardiner opened the first session, which was addressed by Reg Sorensen MP, and on the Sunday Martin Scott spoke about South West Africa and the United Nations Organisation.

At a German weekend, in July, there was some discussion about ways in which German members could help further the aims of International Service on their return to Germany – for instance, by acting as agents in recruiting new members there and by scouting for possible work for new overseas sections.

CHAPTER 5

Getting established – FAUIS at Petersfield and abroad

"COMING UP TO Steep from Petersfield", writes David Hall, "the first impression of Dunannie was of an elegant, if somewhat shabby, period country house.... Inside, the house was full of stairs and corridors. At the back was a large common room with French windows overlooking the garden. Above this was housed the library, which had come with a lot of furniture from Gordon Square. There were outhouses and parking space for HGH (the Bedford truck) and the shooting brake."

He had arrived there following a training camp held at an old RAF camp near Havant in August 1949. "Peter Jackson, the Training Officer, had us running around the site at 5.30 am, and route marching through local streets at 2 in the morning. No doubt the toughening-up process was necessary for the long days of manual work ahead, but it seemed like a pacifist organisation run on military lines." On the other hand, life at Dunannie, he found "was, for the times, and compared with overseas service, comfortable and civilised. The building was crowded, the dormitories were cramped and cold and the washing facilities very limited, but the common room was comfortable and there was always the peace and quiet of the library."

Reveille was at 6 am, and breakfast half an hour later, with porridge and always something cooked, even if it was only fried bread and tomatoes. Mark Chamberlain, who was the first cook quartermaster at Petersfield, had completed the kitchen set-up at

*Training Camp, Havant, 1949: Helmut Abels taking a
German language class.*
(PHOTO: MAURICE BROOMFIELD)

Training Camp, Havant, 1949: an informal music group in a Nissen hut.
(PHOTO: MAURICE BROOMFIELD)

the start of the year and written out a routine for the Aga cooker. After breakfast, it was time for the farm workers to set out so that work could start at 7.30 am. For some, reaching the farms meant a wearying bike ride. By 8 o'clock the house was empty, except for the cooks, cashier and administrator. Between 5 and 6 pm the workers returned, had a bath – which often involved queueing – and a change of clothes. After supper, many just wanted to sit and rest their weary limbs. Some listened to the wireless, others read or wrote letters in the library. Some chatted and smoked; though there was no alcohol at Dunannie, many started smoking there. By 10 pm it was time for lights out. Saturday started like any other working day, but from midday it was the weekend, with time for a visit to the local cinema in Petersfield, to read a Sunday newspaper if you could lay hands on it, or to discuss pacifism, religion, politics, and where the International Service was going. "From time to time", says David Hall, "there were dances, when heavily made-up girls appeared as from nowhere and steered their bashful partners around the floor to the accompaniment of Victor Sylvester and Edmundo Ros, on gramophone records".

Apart from the farming work, there were other sections that operated from Petersfield, some helping to earn money, others just supplying a service. "We successfully tendered for a contract near Chichester", Mike Ellis recalls, "digging trenches for drains. I wonder what the Unions thought?". Gerald Burt was part of a small section that went to the School of Handicrafts in Chertsey, Surrey, doing full-time maintenance work during the day and helping in the children's leisure activities in the evenings. Quaker homes for the elderly at Polegate, Sussex (Bernhard Baron Homes) and Wolverhampton (Woodlands) were also glad to have assistance, usually with short-term maintenance tasks or fill-in help. Denis Earp remembers going to Polegate to do decorating work with Hartmut Weber, one of the first three German members of International Service.

As an affiliated member of the Association of Work Camps, FAUIS was able to co-operate with IVSP in a project at Eltham in September 1949, constructing a playing field for the London Federation of Boys' Clubs, and was also able to send three members to decorate a Church and Youth Club in Clerkenwell.

In October 1949 a small group went to Le Court, a nursing home at Liss run by Leonard Cheshire VC, and the first of what became a nationwide chain of Cheshire Homes. "Life there was fascinating and a little bizarre", writes Simon Cohen. "The matron was very ill with TB and ran the place from her darkened bedroom. The next most experienced nurse decided she would rather cook and, without much experience in that field, took over the kitchen. There was a male nurse with only one leg, and a gardener who practised long Buddhist meditations in a shed. Much of the work was undertaken by the residents, some of whom were suffering from progressive diseases. The atmosphere was nevertheless wonderfully happy and buoyant."

The section helped on the wards, in the kitchen and scullery, and with the office work and driving. "Gifts were always arriving from supporters all over the world", Simon adds. "One day I opened a large tin from New Zealand which I took to contain cooking fat. I fried a pan full of eggs in this only to discover that it was honey!". Mike Ellis, acting as temporary chauffeur at Le Court, recalls driving on Brooklands Racing Track, "albeit in a Jowett Bradford 2-cylinder van", and Ray Ferris was also a driver, going with Group Captain Cheshire to Farnborough every Monday so that he could bring the vehicle back.

Cheshire himself, the spirit behind Le Court, was quite often there. Simon Cohen again: "Our arrival from FAUIS was for him literally an answer to prayer and, as a great war hero, he had no problem in accepting us as COs. Sometimes he would call a staff meeting and address us all like a squadron about to go into battle. He loved to show people the chapel, and I would often see him there early in the morning at prayer. Sometimes we would find a body laid out under a white sheet and I would try to work out which patient had died in the night.... The co-existence of happiness and death there was very inspiring. I think our section gave a lot of support and energy at a crucial time, and each of us certainly gained from our time at Le Court."

In Germany IS was able to continue the work started by PWS. At Cologne a large war-supply wooden hut was re-erected to form a Salvation Army hostel for homeless girls, and there was

Le Court, Liss, 1950: Leonard Cheshire (left) with gifts sent to this first Cheshire Home.

(PHOTO: DAVID HALL)

Rösrath, near Cologne, 1949: Jack Eglon (seated, left), on a visit to the Section, outside one of the half-timbered buildings.

(PHOTO: MARK CHAMBERLAIN)

a further six months work nearby at the Pestalozzi village for orphan children, based on a similar settlement in Switzerland.

Here the group was engaged in restoring damaged buildings and reclaiming land. Rösrath was to become familiar to later IS sections, but when Mark Chamberlain and Gerard Wakeman went there, in March 1949, the barracks that had been housing first for POWs and then for DPs were being converted into family homes for the orphaned children. The work was hard, mainly breaking concrete and draining cess pools, sometimes relieved by work in the fields, sowing crops. On visits to German contacts in Cologne and Düsseldorf, Mark remembers that they had to rely on accommodation found by the Military Government (BAOR) Education Department.

In France too, IS returned to the Catholic orphanage at Vauréal, which PWS had helped establish from semi-derelict property. The work here had opened up requests from the French Red Cross for assistance at other locations in 1950.

Meanwhile there were changes in prospect at Petersfield. Jack Eglon had been travelling in Europe; on his return he began to worry about the success of his ambitions, the future of the organisation, and his own future. After years of modestly paid service with the FAU, he also needed to look to his career as a teacher. With the agreement of the FAU Council, John Swindale took over as General Secretary at the start of 1950, and was joined by Kenneth Hobbs (with the FAU from 1943 to 1946) in March as Administrative Secretary. But the FAU Council also had to look for someone to fill the post of General Secretary more permanently, for John Swindale had planned to leave in July to take up missionary work in Africa. Once again they sought the services of a former member of the FAU. Gerald Gardiner, a member of the General Purposes Committee, approached Jack Norton (FAU 1944-46), who had been in China with the FAU and then the FSU and had stayed on to work with the Agricultural Industry Service, an offshoot of UNRRA. On his return to this country he had become involved in the running of Beltane, a progressive school near Melksham in Wiltshire, but he agreed to take over the young FAUIS in August 1950.

The new General Secretary had a background in educational administration and had served in the war-time FAU, but that was perhaps as far as his similarity to Jack Eglon went. Yet there is little doubt that what be brought into the development of International Service was what was needed at that time. As John Gray says: "We were ambitious and, looking back, I now think that FAUIS did begin to run out of intellectual steam after quite a short while". Colin Henderson, who joined just after Jack Eglon had left and before Jack Norton arrived, comments: "The acting secretaries were trying to establish a sense of purpose within the new organisation. The immediate post-war period was over, but there were still plenty of worthwhile relief projects in Europe. Jack Norton's arrival re-vitalised the organisation. He had lots of ideas, some of them crazy, but many of them good." As for a sense of purpose, the mere survival of FAUIS had become, in a way, a substitute for this.

Raised on a farm, and with a knowledge of agriculture under all sorts of conditions, Jack Norton was well-equipped to re-assess the husbandry and outworking side of the Unit's activities, both of which needed attention. The new ideas included moves towards self-sufficiency, first at Petersfield and then at Melksham, an expansion of earning sections in this country, and a matching expansion of work abroad, for Jack had plenty of contacts and was an industrious negotiator. As a former FAU man he was committed to the "Go Anywhere, Do Anything" philosophy, and he also sought a return to the more democratic ways of the earlier Unit, with sections as autonomous as was practical within an organisation that had a substantially younger membership. Just how successfully an inexperienced and largely unskilled body of young men coped with the extra responsibility may be judged from the following chapters.

CHAPTER 6

Home and away – a profile of FAUIS activity 1950-59

A S THE INTERNATIONAL Service entered its second year
and a new decade dawned, a new pattern of work was
beginning to establish itself. The desire to attract members from
abroad to work alongside members from this country was undi-
minished, but there was recognition that such work should
include giving help to institutions and organisations wherever
relatively unskilled manual labour was useful. The work pool
concept developed at Petersfield to cope with a variety of farming
jobs – during 1949 members worked on over twenty-five different
farms – showed some signs of strain, though it did provide part of
the income that allowed IS to pursue these newer aims. At home
there was a move towards the forestry and hospital work
described in the next chapter. Overseas the emphasis continued
to be on helping with constructional and other work in homes,
settlements and other projects concerned with children and
young people. In Germany the number of young homeless
refugees from the East gave rise to projects like Plön which
seemed to offer longer-term work for the Unit.

In September 1950 there was some talk about whether the
Unit might have a part to play in civilian relief work in Korea,
where the war was in its early stages. At one point the United
Nations Command had been keen to accept a team sent by
Friends (AFSC) alongside Red Cross teams, but their conditions
(that teams should be under military control and should not

report to home committees) were unacceptable. Two months later, the General Secretary, on a visit to Germany, was able to get together with former China colleagues at AFSC's Schloss Kranichstein headquarters to discuss the possibility of work under civilian control, but by then Chinese forces were advancing through North Korea and there was no prospect of an early end to the war.

WORK IN ENGLAND 1950-52

Though often short-term and involving small numbers, the range of new undertakings was certainly varied. A Christmas party for Greek refugee children from the Home at Tilford, complete with a Father Christmas dressed in an RAF flying suit and whiskered and bearded with cotton wool, six weeks of work cleaning and re-decorating a Youth Centre in Clerkenwell, and an Easter project at the Bermondsey Settlement in "an area which the Archbishop of York once referred to as the largest of unbroken poverty in the world"(!) Derek Goodrich wrote of this last: "the main job is the levelling of a bombed area adjoining the Settlement which is about 60 by 35 yards and is to be used as a playground. There is a complete lack of such amenities for the children of the district, as was seen from the vast hordes who descended upon us and tried to help us with varying degrees of success."

A rather longer commitment was the assistance to the Community Association at Lymington, Hampshire, which had acquired a number of ex-WD huts to cope with an energetic programme of activities including film shows, debates, lectures, choral singing,a CAB and clubs for young and old. Four members went to help with the erection of two huts in time for use in the Autumn, but bad weather, a local shortage of cement, and the need for a third hut, kept Christopher Whaite and his team there until March 1951, and he returned in May to put the finishing touches to Friends Court, the name chosen for the quadrangle formed by the newly erected huts.

Quaker facilities, including the Friends International Centre, the Bernhard Baron Homes at Polegate and the 'Woodlands'

Home at Wolverhampton, also provided postings for members during 1950 and 1951, and a team of six, including German and Romanian associate members, went to Swarthmoor Hall in August 1951 to work on improvements to the grounds of this historic Quaker home. The Swarthmoor Hall committee's minutes record: "They are residing in the Hall and giving their service voluntarily upon an unpaid basis, but their maintenance, amounting to about 25s. a week each, is paid for out of the accounts of the Management sub-committee", and subsequently a vote of thanks for the service rendered.

At the end of 1950 Harvard Hospital, near Salisbury, asked whether they could have 20 volunteers for common cold research from mid-January 1951. Although this number was clearly not on, volunteers did go to the Common Cold Research Unit over the next three years; it became a short-term earning section. Roderick Ogley's week there coincided with the death and mourning for King George VI "and thus severely limited radio programmes!".

The Festival of Britain agenda included an International Children's Camp at Loughton, Essex. Six members, four with hospital experience, went there to set up a sick bay, though when Jack Norton visited them there he found them busy on other duties. "Under the direction of Clifford Stanton (FAU 1943-46) field cooking stoves were being made from 50 gallon petrol drums because commercially made models had failed to arrive." The go-anywhere-do-anything tradition was at it again!

Work in 1951 included the development of the new HQ at Lavender Farm, Melksham. Here gardening, the keeping of pigs and poultry, and the establishment of repair shops, both increased the self-sufficiency of the Unit and provided a platform for training new intakes of members in the variety of tasks they might be asked to do.

FRANCE 1950-52

At the start of 1950, five members were at Vauréal, to which the Unit had returned in December 1949. There was still plenty of clearance work in the grounds of the Château. David Lewis wrote: "..There are four large tree-stumps which have to be dug right out of the ground. We are working right down by the banks of the Oise and, in removing one large specimen, dug deeper than the river level and found ourselves working in six inches of water". Winter rains brought flooding on the nearby canal because brushwood on its banks needed clearing, but by the end of January three of the team were able to start work converting the Orangerie into a recreation room for the orphanage children.

"Là haut sur la montagne.."

Work in France was often associated with the efforts of inspired individuals. Robert Ardouvin, a young French ex-Legionnaire working in Paris after the war had set up "Les Amis des Enfants de Paris", an organisation dedicated to housing, rehabilitating and resettling homeless children, often to be found living in goods yards and railway stations. Plans included a hostel in Paris and a centre in the provinces where children could live under home-like conditions, be educated and learn a trade of their choosing. In 1949 Les Amis were given a house and land in the deserted mountain village of Vercheny-le-Vieux in the Vercors region. Its inhabitants had been forced to abandon it because of soil erosion – as the song goes "les neiges and les rochers étaient unis pour l'arracher" – and had moved down into the valley, but Ardouvin and his volunteers began to clear the site and dig into the hillside for water. David Lewis visited it in March 1951 and found a small settlement hard at work. Everyone called everyone else 'tu' and 'toi' and he was greeted by "salut camarade" rather than "bonjour monsieur". The life was very simple but the atmosphere was good and, following his report, it was decided to establish a section there.

Those who served at Vercheny worked long hours at very arduous tasks but are united in appreciating the very good spirit of the community. By May 1951 a team of five, under Section Leader Roddy Blackburn, was settling in well, and reported: "Frank Lees and David Hall have been repairing the damage to the roof of their house caused by recent storms; John Whitney has been blowing up a house to make way for a road and in quiet

Vercheny, 1950: hard work on unpromising terrain.
(PHOTO: DAVID HALL)

moments he has been working on the land." Most of the work was connected with the water supply, cutting out a reservoir. Here explosives could not be used for fear of disturbing the water table. The section was still at it in September, when Colin Henderson arrived there: "The work was physically hard and our section (swelled by many international volunteers during the summer months) spent months hacking away at the mountain-side with picks and shovels to reach a source of water. During non-working hours we were surrounded by children whose need had brought them to this Pestalozzi-style community." After his return to England, he writes "I often wondered what had happened to this idealistic project. So in 1990, with my wife, I paid a visit. Remarkably, several people who had been prominent in the community when we left were still there. We were entertained to lunch by Robert Ardouvin, though sadly conversation was limited by our lack of French. It gave me a great sense of pleasure and fulfilment however to find that not only was the village thriving, but the work we had done forty years earlier was still bearing fruit. Robert showed me the water supply piped from 'la source' where we had worked so hard in 1950".

At the end of the year severe winter weather brought outdoor work at Vercheny to a standstill. Les Amis was closing its Paris office and bringing all its personnel to Vercheny for the winter months, so the FAUIS section withdrew. In the end AEP decided it could not make use of volunteer help the following summer, bringing to an end what had been felt to be one of the best IS undertakings on the Continent.

Sections in Northern France

Meanwhile, still in France but nearer home, there were other requests to be met. La Baronne Mallet was establishing a new centre at Coye la Forêt, near Chantilly, for about 60 young children who were permanently injured in the war or were otherwise infirm. This was a link with PWS work done earlier at Château Mesnuls, also for Oeuvres en Faveur des Enfants Mutilés Victimes de la Guerre, of which Baronne Mallet was vice-president. In fact when work at Coye la Forêt turned out to be less and of shorter duration than expected – reconstructing and painting a gymnasium – some members of the section moved on to Mesnuls. Others stayed to paint about 120 beds and stools for the bedrooms and stain 60 stools and several tables for the dining room. "Without the Section the Château could not have opened" said Baronne Mallet in thanking FAUIS at the opening of the home in July 1950.

Another smaller section at Perrier sur Andelle, near Rouen, was based at a privately-run orphanage set up originally by Mlle.Harel after the First World War and since used as a holiday home for children sent to her by the Securité Sociale – children, Frank Lees noted "in similar circumstances to those the Vercheny children were in. Now, as the Securité Sociale is behind in its payments, she has broken with it, and still using her own money, intends to take the same children for longer periods until they are eleven." Frank asked her to contact Vercheny, as their aims were similar. At Perrier, David Gray remembers "repainting the exterior (in January!) of the large house with its concertina window-grilles".

Vacances Familiales Ouvrière stemmed from the work of the Abbé Godin, as Frank Lees says "a modern saint and workman priest", who died in 1944. Its aim was to provide centres where workmen who could not otherwise afford it could come to spend their holidays with their families. Derrick Smith and Dennis Tomlin went to do plumbing, electrical and decoration work at the Tannay Rest Home in January 1951. After Easter,Colin Henderson, who had been working with David Gray at Perriers, replaced Derrick, who was having further trouble at home with the Ministry of Labour. At the end of April the Home was opened to families and the section closed, returning with a letter of appreciation from Louis Godin, a directeur of the Home and brother of the Abbé.

David Gray was lucky enough to be sent, with others, to help with re-painting and re-plastering work at the AFSC's newly bought Centre Quaker Internationale in Avenue Mozart, Paris, in April 1951. "Six weeks of Paris in the Spring! Fantastic!"

But he also enjoyed the company of AFSC staff and learned how to apply "Enduit", an oil-based clay for clammy, crumbling wall plaster. And he recalls hearing General de Gaulle speak in the Bois de Boulogne – big man, big voice. From Paris he joined Walter Martin (Section Leader), Helmut Abels and Hugh Jepson at the AFSC Foyer des Jeunes in Saint Nazaire, Brittany, where the twin jobs were building a "terrain des sports" and helping with house-moving for bombed-out citizens returning to rebuilt homes.

In the meantime Henri van Etten, a Dutch Quaker and an earlier IS contact, had asked for help at his Centre de Ré-education (a sort of open-doors Borstal) in the Château Beuzevillette, near Le Havre. A section of six members went there in August 1951, under Section Leader Bernard Parfrement. David Gray again: "The work was rebuilding the interior of the top floor of the château to make it into additional dormitory space for the 'borstal boys'. Many of them were already in residence there and worked with us as 'builders' mates' occasionally." The boys were aged 13-16, all of them sent to Beuzevillette by the law courts in Le Havre, who believed that these particular boys would be reformed by a loving but firm community. No locks and no fence or wall, David noted, and indeed earlier plans for FAUIS to help with building a wall around the estate had been dropped because of this policy. It was, he recalls, a happy and successful venture, and "we learned a lot from them and made some personal friendships, being not too far from their ages." When, in later life, David, then at Woodbrooke, went on teaching tours in France, French Quakers would say to him "You speak English like an Oxford man, but you speak French like a docker from Le Havre!".

Towards the end of October 1951, Jack Norton and Dennis Tomlin set out for France, Jack as part of a tour of overseas sections, and Dennis en route for Champcevrais as the first member of a new section. They travelled from Southampton to Le Havre, calling first at Beuzevillette. Jack had intended to return to Melksham before going on to Germany, but at Beuzevillette there was a three-day holiday for the boys and the section had been lent a Peugeot van, so the opportunity to extend his stay with a visit to the experimental farming community at de Bouron seemed too good to miss. He reported later in Occasional Information: "Henri Schultz, his mother, wife and two sons, conceived the idea of a farming community with an international membership witnessing peace and guided broadly by Quaker principles. They are practical people seeking to be practical about their Christianity and being not a little successful. Despite four years of extremely hard going, during which they had used all their savings, the Schultz family had steered the experiment with unfailing faith and hope. There was that unmistakable air of strength and confidence." Though appalled at Henri's account of French landlord-tenant law, Jack was obviously impressed with the experiment, not least because of the community's efforts to become self-sufficient. Three more members were sent to join Dennis Tomlin, and effectively Champcevrais became the FAUIS French section for the next three and a half years. In the summer of 1952, when there were work-campers available to lend a hand with the community's tasks, the section withdrew, but returned there in mid-September, while Henri Schultz on a rare trip to England to attend the Friends World Conference at Oxford, visited Melksham and proffered advice on work at Lavender Farm.

Richard Brown joined the new section at Champcevrais in mid-November 1951, and has kept a detailed account written in letters home: "The château (de Bouron) is an enormous farmhouse... and it was once surrounded by a moat. There are several other farm buildings, also old, nearby...also another smaller château and some houses in the village included in the land rented by the community, which is legally an agricultural co-operative. Both buildings and land have been badly neglected...". Of the community, he writes: "There are about 20 people in the Communauté, besides ourselves.....formed around two families with several others, Swiss, Belgian, Dutch and French, and led by Henri Schultz....The full members of the community have few personal possessions, and due to the need for capital development, no pocket money. However the food is very plentiful and good, and laundry is done in the house, not in the river." The food included "a lot of apples, mainly stewed, as there are a great many apple trees in the orchard. Peeling apples is as regular a kitchen job as peeling spuds." Henri Schultz, he writes, "is very impressive when he starts talking about the Communauté movement. He has less to do with the day-to-day running of the Community than with the movement in general and with French Quakers..."

Work at Champcevrais was hard but rewarding. Jack Norton noted, on a second visit there in March 1952, that it was based on a sixty-six hour week, though many members of the community worked even more.

GERMANY 1950-52

Jack Norton's visits in Germany in November 1951 were to Köln-Brück, where a section of 4 was still working, and to Plön, from which the Unit had recently withdrawn.

It was in April 1950 that 5 members first went to Plön, in Schleswig-Holstein, to work in co-operation with the Salvation Army on a hostel for homeless and workless young people, mostly refugees. The Seehof consisted of a large house and range of farm buildings on an estate sloping down to the See, one of the many lakes in the district. A site next to the house had been prepared for a Swedish prefabricated building to provide a home for the director of the colony. At the same time the range of farm buildings was to be developed as dormitories, recreation and training rooms. Major Preece, Public Relations Officer for the Salvation Army in Western Germany, was supervising the project and made the preliminary arrangements for the IS team, which then tackled the digging of a cellar for the new house. While awaiting its arrival from Sweden, the section still managed to keep busy, and Gerard Wakeman wrote: "The main achievement of the week has been the building of the hen-house; Donn (Webb) and myself have been working on this with Herr Plischke, who is the 'Fachman' here. Though none of us has had any experience of brick-laying before, the work progressed satisfactorily and the result is nothing to be ashamed of. Joe (Sturge) has continued steadily with the construction of toilets and now has three and a half to his credit...". The Salvation Army invited the section to attend an International Youth Camp at Kiel, and Joe and Dennis Stubbs spent some time there. Colin Reed, who joined the section not long after, had an unpleasant accident when he fell through a ceiling hatch onto a concrete floor, fractured a lumbar vertebra, and was faced with twelve weeks in plaster at the Kreis Krankenhaus at Preetz. Simon Cohen, who replaced him writes: "We slept at the top of the barn from which he had fallen. I was mostly employed painting the director's Swedish house or acting as plumber's mate to Dennis Stubbs. His knowledge of German was even less than mine, but when we went into Plön to buy brackets or pipes he always got what he wanted by pointing and asking for 'eins von denen'....Talking to the German tradesmen on the site, I was shocked to hear them say that Hitler had not been so bad. He had given them houses and jobs, they said."

Work on the Swedish house progressed well enough for it to be completed before the winter of 1950-51. Just as well, for hard weather in January held up work and doesn't seem to have done the section's morale much good. Ian Trott, posted there at the beginning of the month, recalls: "Our labour was used in a variety of ways, mainly rebuilding a shed block and working in the fields. As an exercise in giving relief and helping international relations, it was an unmitigated disaster. We had little respect for the major running the project, and he saw us in much the same way as he saw the East German refugees who worked alongside us."

Be that as it may, by summer things had got back to normal, and work had started on the erection of a greenhouse before the section was withdrawn. At the time of Jack's visit it did not seem likely that there would be a return to Plön, but in fact a small section under the experienced Donn Webb, on his second visit, went back for three months in the Spring of 1952. Colin Henderson found himself "moving large quantities of glass from Plön to the Seehof by tractor and trailer, and digging holes to look for pipes buried by previous sections." Work on the Kinderheim and hostel was by then almost complete.

Work at Köln-Brück started just a year after that at Plön, with a section consisting of Alan Cox, Ted Dyson, John Midgley and Donn Webb helping Aufbaudienst, a small co-operative of home-builders in this suburb of the city. Originally formed by homeless ex-service men and their families, who contributed labour and received a local government grant, Aufbaudienst had an ambitious target of 120 homes. The estate, as Jack Norton noted on his visit, was literally being built on sand; digging to a depth of seven feet involved lifting and moving hundreds of tons of sand. The two-storey houses, each occupied by two families, were being built with reclaimed bricks from bombed buildings and were of a high standard of workmanship. Ray Ferris remembers that "all through the summer and autumn we laboured every day from 7 am to 5 pm digging out cellars for the houses. Food was spartan, most of our meals consisting of rye bread, margarine and poor jam. Supper was often noodles and soup." Hans Hens was the boss, and "sharp at seven every Saturday morning Herr Hens called on us. We dragged ourselves from bed and accompanied him on the long tram ride through streets of endless rubble to the city centre and our weekly cleansing at the city swimming pool".

Donn Webb was Section Leader at Köln-Brück for most of the year's work there. One of the things he remembers is "the day that Don White shot a German civilian through his hat with an airgun pellet (not a very appropriate action for a pacifist). The German called the police who were waiting for me when I got back – my colleagues had made the police understand that I was Section Leader and they couldn't answer for Don White's actions! When the police saw me I don't think they thought this young guy could possibly be the leader, and in the end shrugged it off by telling the German that they couldn't act because we were English; he was very disgruntled. Don wasn't allowed any guns after that." By Easter 1952 the project was more secure, in that it was receiving enough financial aid and could muster its own work-force; by then too a new opportunity for work had arisen nearby – a return to Rösrath.

WORK IN ENGLAND FROM 1952 ONWARD

With the expansion of the programme of work in hospital and forestry sections and the move towards self-sufficiency at Lavender Farm, there were fewer opportunities to supply other work at home. Some short-term work continued – the supply of volunteers to the Common Cold Research Unit, for instance.

This was David Maxwell's first assignment, in 1954: "We were given slightly unpleasant nose drops, supposed to give us colds, and lived in pairs isolated from others to have our health checked daily." Roger Bush, also there in 1954, writes: "The huts were warm and food was delivered to the door in insulated containers. Perhaps I was chosen as one of the controls – I don't recall having a cold there. We were allowed into the neighbouring countryside as long as we avoided any risk of infection. On one occasion I encountered a fellow out shooting, with his dog, and, unarmed as I was, had to ask him to keep his distance." Not long after, common cold research at Harvard Hospital came to an end, to be replaced by research into influenza. Two teams of four members each took part in tests for the new programme.

Other home sections of relatively short duration included gardening and general help at two homes for the elderly – at Ifield Park, near Crawley, and for a second time at Woodlands Home, near Wolverhampton.

Building alteration and maintenance work was taken on at Walton Elm School in Marnhull, near Sturminster Newton, Dorset, a posting Ian Trott remembers as enjoyable: "My main occupation was as an odd job man reglazing the windows after the many breakages caused by the disturbed children. It also gave me the opportunity to work with the children, though my discipline was a far cry from the 'do as you like' policy adopted by the school. However we adapted to each other eventually...". Enjoyable maybe, but Basil Mogridge found painting other than ground floor windows had an element of hazard: "To be at the top of a ladder painting second storey windows is one thing, but when a maladjusted child with an odd sense of humour is at the bottom of the ladder, the matter acquires a different aspect." Maintenance work he also found had been "widely interpreted to include not merely decorating and minor repairs, but also such things as taking PT, camps, prayers, giving piano lessons, supervising meals...". The first section went to Walton Elm in the summer of 1952, and the third and last left in September 1953.

Work at the FSC/Oxford Committee for Famine Relief warehouse in London started in 1952. Typically a section of two helped with sorting and baling at St Barnabas Church Hall in Pimlico Road, a large gloomy building in which gifts of clothing accumulated at a rate that often hid the windows. At the back of the Hall was a huge, unstable, mountain of shoes sent in, many of them virtually useless. Accommodation was at Millwood House, Ladbroke Grove, where Helen and Marjorie Thomas ran a boarding house which was an agreeable home to FAUIS personnel working in London, and made this a popular section despite the humdrum nature of the job. Later, in 1957, Alan Quilley stayed there while acting as driver of the ambulance used by the National Association of the Paralysed to take patients to Broadstairs for week-long holidays during the summer. This was a duty well in keeping with the Unit's name, and was first undertaken the previous year; before that, in 1954 and 1955 members also helped out at a NAP holiday camp at Tankerton.

Another regular section worked with OCFR in Oxford itself. For Roderick Ogley, who was there in 1953, it was "particularly pleasant (and rewarding, in that for the last three months...I was encouraged in a trial run of what was to be my post-FAU job – North of England Appeals Organiser). It was also through OCFR's Director, Leslie Kirkley, my boss there, that a few years later, when no longer its employee, I met my wife". Roger Bush writes: "I know I was in Oxford at the time when the first sub-four-minute mile was run by Roger Bannister. I had even intended to watch his attempt at the Iffley Road sports ground, less than a quarter of a mile from the YMCA hostel which housed members of the section, but can only claim to have heard the distant cheering that signalled his success." Of the work, he recalls that it was split between assistance at the Gift Shop in Broad Street and office work at some rented premises in Cornmarket where the all-important index of subscribers was kept. "In those days of low technology there was no photocopier, and the risk to the still-young charity of losing its valuable records in a fire was a real one. So teams of North Oxford ladies and others came in as volunteers to copy the cards by hand and create a duplicate index which could be housed elsewhere."

Some home section work was highly seasonal, like that of the three-member section in June-September at the Bromsgrove Grass Dryers Association. This was possibly the most physically taxing job undertaken in this country, all members and their replacements suffering temporarily disabling injury after working very long hours under difficult conditions. Another seasonal job, rather more agreeable, was building and running a stand shared with the National Peace Council at the Schoolboys' Own Exhibition held in London in the first two weeks of 1957. The feature of the stand was an electrically operated quiz machine constructed in the workshops at Melksham and offering a choice of four answers to sixteen questions of general and social interest. According to the Annual Report nearly 30,000 visitors called at the stand, despite the rival attractions of the armed forces' exhibits.

In these later years of the FAUIS, the move from Melksham to Chalfont St Peter provided on-the-spot labouring work. Peter Leeming, Philip Brown and Howard Brunton remember particularly the putting in of a 6ft pre-cast concrete fence around Tunmers (see Chapter 9).

AND FURTHER ABROAD, 1952 ONWARDS

In France the connection with the de Bouron community at Champcevrais continued. Keith Newson, who was there in the early part of 1952, writes that he became part of this "extraordinary family of blood relations and numerous neurotic asylumseekers from the rigours of post-war life on the Continent". Though he learnt French, how to lay a hedge, press cider and prepare blood sausages, he reflects: "I think this experience convinced me that this kind of communal life was a recipe for disaster, but it was nevertheless unfailingly enjoyable. Don't ask me what good the FAUIS did for the Community; I suppose we helped rehabilitate a tiny portion of rural France."

By 1954 the Annual Report noted: "Although the agricultural work with the Communauté de Bouron cannot be regarded as in the field of relief or reconstruction, it has been a unique opportunity to share the life and work of a small group dedicated to peace as a way of life.... Unfortunately, the lease of the farming land....will expire in May 1955 and cannot be renewed. It is not yet clear whether a new home will be found nor whether there will be a continuing opportunity for us to share their concerns." The section withdrew in February 1955, but the Communauté did indeed find another home, and by Spring a small section of three members was on its way to Avaray, in the Loire Valley, in the belief (which proved ill-founded) that the work there would be more appropriate to the Unit's proper functions.

Here the former inhabitants of de Bouron were getting to grips with an environment very different from that of Champcevrais. At Avaray there was the somewhat decayed moated château to deal with, but the grounds, though neglected, were very fruitful – this was The Garden of France. The owner of the château, a Monsieur Mauve, had agreed to the development of an international camping ground in the meadows below the terraced gardens. This forced redundancy on the small flock of sheep there, some of which went to the kitchen to supply meat to go with the abundant vegetables.

In the château itself there was much work to be done in restoring the two salons and painting and papering the many bedrooms. Hardly was this work finished than there was an invasion of not one, but two, colonies de vacances. The population of the château was suddenly swelled by flocks of young French teenage girls, some from families who had just left Algeria, then still a French province – just. This did wonders for the section's speed in learning the language. Meanwhile the gardens and orchards were being tamed, the hay harvest gathered, and the important water pipeline laid for the proposed camping ground. Excavating for a new drain near to the gatehouse facing Avaray village, someone uncovered a skull, from its square shape reckoned to be Prussian, from the Franco-Prussian War. This view was supported by the further discovery of a spike from a Pickelhelm.

For relaxation there were bathing trips to the Loire, about a mile away (just about opposite today's Avaray nuclear power station), and outings in the camionette to visit some of the grander châteaux, including the early "son et lumière" spectacle at Chambord.

FAUIS was still represented by a small section at Avaray into the following year, by which time the camping ground was ready for its first full season, but the Unit then recognised that the work was inappropriate to it and withdrew. During the summer of 1956 attention switched to supporting work-camps of the Brethren Service Commission, the Mennonite Voluntary Service and Nothilfergemeinschaftdienst der Freunde in Austria and Germany, where the main activity was that of helping refugees to build their homes.

A further section saw service in France in 1957 when they were sent to help Abbé Pierre's Sans Abri organisation in Lyons, where nearly 4000 people, many of them North Africans, were without proper shelter. The work was the building of simple but adequate housing. Euan Pearson, who was there with Bob Culling (Section Leader), Nicholas Evens and John Drage, in September and October, went back to Lyons the following year after leaving FAUIS, stayed for almost a year, learnt French and later went on to study Cinema in Paris, becoming a documentary film maker.

In Germany, the return to Rösrath in 1952 found the premises formerly occupied by the Pestalozzi settlement, where PWS and IS members had worked before, now a residential hostel for young refugees and run by the Evangelical Church. The Jugendheim, Nick Hudson wrote: "is approached by various roads through the forest, only partially metalled and badly pot-holed. The home itself is on a site which has been used for many purposes since it was first built on in 1911. In the 1914-18 war it was used as an artillery training school... balloons were employed to hoist the officers to points of vantage, and the concrete foundations of the winches are still here. In 1934 it became an army barracks again, and 2000 troops were housed in wooden huts, all now destroyed. At the outbreak of war it became a prison camp and was occupied by English, French, American and finally Russian POWs. After the war Polish DPs moved in, and then the Pestalozzi – it was then that the former FAU section worked here. Owing to managerial disputes, Pestalozzi handed over as a going concern to the Evangelical Church.... The main building is a big stucco house facing a court 75 yards square. This is bounded by new buildings of half-timbered construction, black and white, all bungalow or ground floor and attic." The inhabitants fell into two categories – children aged 7 to 12 who went to school and 17-24 year olds, mostly working at trades·in the district with a view to becoming independent.

Hugh Hebert writes: "There were usually six of us...Nick Hudson, section leader, Chris Browne, Ted Milborrow, Colin Sorensen, Kenneth Adams, and me. We worked under the direction of the camp foreman/handyman Herr Grützenbach, a small wiry middle-aged Rhinelander with a flat, round, freckled face, a nose that scarcely disturbed the plane of his cheeks. He had a big grin, ginger hair and virtually no English... He was cheerful, tolerant and shrewd. He was the kind of boss we needed to turn a bunch as disparate as us into a reasonably effective unit. We laboured, repaired, cannibalised timber from some of the ruined huts, did whatever basic tasks were needed..... It didn't seem much to have come all this way to do." That was until they got the big project – the building of the Fahrradschuppen, the bicycle shed, important to the boys, who owned maybe 50 bikes and had

nowhere to store them. "Later members of the section" says
Hugh "were to help on a more uplifting task, building the chapel.
The monument we completed while I was a member of the
section was simple, practical, defiantly secular. But it was no
ordinary bike shed. Herr Grützenbach wanted it built in a way
that fitted in with the better huts around, and these were built the
way the Elizabethans built. Maybe it was the only way he knew.
So we built a half-timbered bike shed, perhaps 10 metres square
– big baulks of cannibalised timber with brick or breeze and mor-
tar infill, a pitched roof...". While there, Hugh was conscious of
the gulf between the section and the Jugendheim youths that
seemed too wide to bridge with inadequate common language,
and felt guilty about it, but comments: "Later, on reflection, I
thought perhaps the bike shed was more important than an
acquaintance scraped out of a sense of obligation. We belonged to
a nation that had helped destroy their families and their homes.
Their half-timbered Fahrradschuppen was at least a solid statement that some of the British had come to build and not to
demolish."

Nick Hudson remembers the songs: "Jup (Herr
Grützenbach) and I used to specialise in singing: 'Bravo, Bravo,
beinah wie Caruso' ('nicht schön, aber laut', Jup used to say of
our din)", but also the more serious side of things. "What I really
learnt in Germany was, astonishingly, belief in the future. Like
many of us I was extremely pessimistic about the future, forward
planning seemed pointless. Yet here were these kids, refugees
from the East, who had lost almost everything, but were saving in
the hope of being able to buy a secondhand bicycle 'in eighteen
months'. By the end of my time there I believed in the future
again."

During March and April 1955 a group of members went to
North Germany to take part in work camps organised by the
Internationaljugendgemeinschaftdienst (IJGD – pronounced ee-
yot-gay-day). "Our joining instructions" writes one "were to
catch the boat train to Harwich, cross to Hook of Holland and
proceed by train to Bremen, where we would get further directions. The sea crossing was rough, many were sick, and the
Netherlands landscape bleak and unwelcoming. On arrival at

Bremen the further directions were missing. Some frantic tele-phoning eventually established that our next destination was Delmenhorst, a Saxon town reeking of the linoleum that was its major industry. There we were met by our German hosts and conducted to a briefing seminar at Steinkimmen, not far distant. Hardly had we arrived when snow fell so heavily it might as well have been a hundred miles away..". Malcolm Page wrote, for Occasional Information: "The Jugendhof was set in pine woods, in a flat featureless landscape, without another house in sight. We began with a four-day seminar to learn about the problems of East German refugees, and to discuss the camps. We learned that the big majority of young refugees who cross do so for personal and social reasons, not political ones...We were told that we must introduce the East Germans to the idea of playing for playing's sake, explain what doing something genuinely voluntarily means, and to introduce them to democracy through camp self-govern-ment, which they would find difficult as they are accustomed to taking orders. Finally we were told we must give the East Germans 'joy and courage'."

From Steinkimmen, four members went to a camp at Misburg, a suburb of Hannover. Roger Bush was one of them: "We were supposed to be laying the foundations for a refugee camp, but again the weather took a hand; the ground in this frozen suburb of the Saxon capital was so hard that it could only be broken with a pick-axe.....A sudden thaw brought a new set of problems: the lorries laden with hardcore either stuck on the edge of the site or their loads sank into the mud. Here, for once, FAUIS forestry experience came to the rescue; we were able to dig our diagonal drains and build a maintainable road surface into the heart of the site. Even the young refugees, a hardbitten lot, were impressed."

David Whitworth wrote in a letter home: "Have I told you that we are working with German convicts? They are a special type of convict however; they are all in prison for having been drunk in charge of a car.... it does give the work an atmosphere to be watched by armed guards. The prisoners seem to be rather amused that we have got the worst work (they are house building) – I do not feel so amused."

The section was treated to some visits to see the recovering industries of Saxony: to Bahlsen to see the birth of the Leibnizkek, to Hanomag's tractor factory, Continental tyres, and a coach trip to Wolfsburg to see the longest production line in Europe turning out Volkswagen beetle-cars.

A further IJGD work-camp to which some members went was on the island of Juist. "'In Östfriesland they all speak Platdeutsch' said our German hosts, 'very like English, so you will understand them'. Crossing to Juist from Norddeich, it seemed to be little more than a sandbank writ large. The youth hostel where the camp was housed had a problem: the encroaching sand dunes kept burying it. It was our job to dig it out. This we would do energetically all week, and at the weekend storm winds would spring up and drive all the sand back onto the site. As to the Platdeutsch, it was hard to test the predictions about it; the few natives were extremely taciturn and seemed to communicate mainly in grunts and with gestures. Maybe the wind had something to do with it." Most of those who worked on these camps, and others at Altenau in the Harz and Edersee near Kassel, enjoyed hospitality with German families before returning to England or going on to other work on the Continent.

Brethren and Mennonite work-camps during the Summer of 1957 also gave the opportunity to meet and work with young people of other nationalities. A MVS camp at Buitenpost, Holland helped with the reconstruction of a Protestant church; in camps at Elixhausen, Mitterbach and Waiern in Austria the work was on refugee housing projects initiated by the Evangelical Church; and in Madrid, Spain, the support of the MVS had been enlisted by a Jesuit Father concerned for the welfare of the Andalucian peasant community who had arrived in the city in search of jobs and had settled in conditions of squalor.

A work camp in Algeria was more problematical. Service Civil International and the IVSP were helping to build an Arab village school outside Algiers, but the camp had largely collapsed when French participation was withdrawn because of the escalation of the Algerian 'war'. This was May 1956 and probably the nearest that FAUIS came to working in a war zone. After a

request for help, Howard Brunton and Martin Samuels enter-
prisingly got in Marseilles the visas that were impossible to obtain
in London. This success was unfortunately followed by Howard's
arrest in Algiers by local police when he was with the Swiss SCI
organiser, who had with him reports on the situation in Algeria.
Interrogated for several hours by the French equivalent of Special
Branch, who were convinced that anything to do with SCI was a
communist plot, he found himself trying to explain that the work
camp was non-political, having to give a detailed explanation of
FAUIS, its aims, who joined it, how it was recognised by the
British government, relations with SCI and so on. He was asked
to sign a lengthy statement, but his passport was not returned to
him, and though he and Martin, who joined him subsequently,
were able to work at the Bel Air camp in Hussein-Dey for a
few weeks, they were subsequently expelled from the country,
following the expulsion of Emil Tanner of SCI. Expulsion from
Algeria at that time meant expulsion from France, where the Unit
had continuing work, and it took nearly a year for the order
against Howard to be cancelled – in part through the efforts of
Philip Noel-Baker (FAU World War 1), then at the Foreign
Office.

It would be wrong to conclude without mention of the individual secondments and the AFSC scholarships which took
members outside Europe.

William Rowley spent most of his time in the FAUIS working
with the FSC in Rasulia, India, where his skill with things
mechanical was very welcome (he had previously trained as a jig
and tool draughtsman at Austin Motors) and he had responsibility for using and maintaining agricultural machinery and vehicles. Not that that was all. "I should make it clear that I have
much more to do than look after three vehicles. A few farmers
round here have pumping sets which they use and abuse for irri-
gating their crops. These and their owners cause quite a lot of
trouble, partly because they do not know how to use the machinery properly. I have come to the conclusion that India is not the
place for a perfectionist. So long as these things work the sun
shines, no one bothers how." One of his reports home contains an
account of a tiger hunt: "They have not been too close – about 20

miles away – but what makes it exciting is that people we know have been involved with them. Three of them had been worrying the cattle near Makeria, a village on the edge of the jungle where we have a farm. They have been around for a month, and people were getting rather fed up with having their cattle killed, so decided to have a drive....Men with guns were spaced along the road and the beaters were moving through the jungle towards them, making as much noise as they could. One of the men had an old muzzle loader gun which was licensed for crop protection; he was stationed at a place where a dry river crossed the road. Much to his surprise and astonishment he saw a tiger come round a bend about 20 yards away. He let the tiger have all he had got and knocked it down. All the other men heard the shot and came running....The leader of the hunt had just got there when he saw the tiger twitch his ears and try to get up, so he shot it dead at close range." William saw the skin the next day. The owner of the gun which first drew blood had to report himself to the DC, as it was not licensed for game – "It is best to report yourself in such cases as usually a lenient view is taken. Not so if someone reports you. All the DC said was 'Good work; try and get the rest if you can'."

Despite post-Suez prospects of work in the Middle East, the only other posting East of Suez seems to have been that of David Morrish, who went out to Tehran in 1958 to work with the UN's Food and Agriculture Organisation. That was in the days of the Shah. David writes of a "spiritual shuffle between Friends Meeting (on Friday), lunch with a local mullah anxious to explore inter-faith views, and visits to the Anglican bishop at Isfahan. The Shah's Iran had its dark side but there was a level of toleration....I have felt in a very personal way the recent rise of fundamentalism in that wonderful country." Only the year before, David had been chosen to lead a section supplying ambulance services to both Greek and Turkish communities in Cyprus along a road that separated the two zones. Here was a further prospect of working in a situation of conflict. Funds were raised for the ambulance, and a team with driving, vehicle maintenance, and first aid experience was selected. Enthusiasm was high, but unfortunately the project, which had the support of Sir Hugh

Foot, the Governor, ran into opposition from the military forces, and was stopped before it could be started.

Four members were awarded UNESCO scholarships enabling them to take part in educational projects organised by AFSC in Mexico. Tom Campbell was the first, in 1953, followed by Anthony Wilson in 1954, David Taylor in 1955 and David Jeffrey in 1957. All wrote lively accounts for Occasional Information. Here is Tom Campbell, encountering an unusual problem: they could get no co-operation from the local villagers on the building of the road – "We talked to the Agente and he promised that twenty men would appear tomorrow, but it was always Manana... ..working alone was having a demoralising effect on our group... As we got accepted more and more into the community, news as to the real reason for the lack of co-operation percolated through. There are four opposition parties in the village. One of the promises of the PRI in the last election was the building of the road. The other parties did not relish implementing their opponents' election programme, and it must have appeared to them that we were in some way linked up with the party in power. We lived in the Senator's house, our invitation came from the Governor, and in our political innocence were continually associating with the party officials..... We were further dissatisfied when the Agente informed us of the new plan for providing labour on the road. The military were to come and force the reluctant to work at bayonet point. He seemed unmoved at our protests and went his way assuring us that this was the customary practice. I thought of another country and its salt mines. The next morning thirty soldiers arrived in the village, but our fears were removed when they took picks and shovels instead of rifles from their trucks....".

And a cheerful P.S from David Taylor: "You know, it's just struck me – the FAU is a good thing, isn't it? Here's Tony Bristow talking about the economics of Thessaly and Kephalonia, Malcolm Page learning German refugee problems, myself talking about conditions of Otomi Indians in Mexico, William Rowley and his tigers, others learning Dutch, French and German. We do at least learn – which I suppose is what life is for."

CHAPTER 7

Hospital and forestry work

QUITE EARLY IN the life of the International Service it became apparent that income from subscriptions, dona- tions and grants was never going to be enough to meet the costs of setting up and maintaining overseas sections. For a body with the word "ambulance" in its title, hospital work looked like offer- ing the best possibility of useful, paid, employment, through which home sections could make a bigger contribution to the IS budget. The background of farming and labouring jobs carried out by the work pool at Petersfield also pointed to opportunities in forestry.

HOSPITALS

Negotiations with the health service and its unions took time. Until well into 1950 the only medical work was down to the volunteers who went to Hammersmith Hospital's Post-Graduate Medical School to take part in experiments on healthy bone marrow as part of the search into a cure for pernicious anaemia and leukaemia or as guinea pigs to the Common Cold Research Unit at Harvard Hospital near Salisbury.

At last, in September 1950, Alan Cox, Brian Bowmer and John Midgley were able to put on their ward orderly coats at St Peter's Hospital, Chertsey. Though clearly the arrangement was satisfactory, for Matron agreed to it continuing into 1951, it called for some rapid adjustments on the part of the pioneer team. John Midgley wrote at the time: "We found it tiring, both mentally and physically, at first.... One feels a constant pressure and awareness of the hierarchy of Matron and Sister and each petty authority a step higher on the ladder of promotion – so different from the friendly feeling of equality to be found in the Unit, where everyone has responsibility and self-respect. Here, one is expected to bear no responsibility but obey orders implicitly – a stultifying semi-military atmosphere."

The work at Chertsey – bedmaking, bedpan and bottle rounds, treatment to prevent bedsores, errands to X-ray departments and path. labs, serving and clearing meals – was echoed in subsequent hospital sections. Brook General Hospital, Shooters Hill, and Bradford Royal Infirmary, were added in 1951. Though student nurses took over the responsibilities of the Chertsey section in March 1952, a new section at Thornbury Hospital, Bristol kept the number of members in hospital service constant, and requests from other hospitals gave prospects for expansion. In some the work reflected the special nature of the hospital: Thornbury was mainly geriatric and St Wulstan's, Malvern Wells, a long-term commitment to which started in November 1952, was a former US Army hut hospital and devoted to the treatment of tuberculosis. By the end of 1952 a fifth hospital section had been established at Wokingham, and income from work done by members was almost matching that from subscriptions and donations. Hospital wages in 1958, the last full year of FAUIS, totalled £13,455, three-quarters of all income and at that time supporting overseas relief work at Linz and Vienna in Austria and Nuremburg in Germany.

Aside from the basic nursing and patient care techniques that members learned at hospital sections there was much value in the contact with staff and patients that the work there gave to those who came from sheltered backgrounds or had joined the Unit fresh from school. Of Bradford RI David Gray writes: "We all picked up some human wisdom from our patients – many ex-miners and many mill-workers – from an urban West Riding city community." And Michael Pittard, also at Bradford, notes that in those days "the ethnic minorities consisted of Latvians, Estonians, Lithuanians and Poles". Among his other recollections were "Bowling Tide, when all the mills closed and for the only time in my six months it was possible to see across the city", and "Ward 3, which had previously been a female ward and in consequence had a surplus of stainless steel bedpans and insufficient glass urinals (bottles). The latter could be augmented by placing two non-matching portions of a broken urinal in the breakages box, but I discovered no way of getting rid of surplus bedpans". Michael comments that nothing changes: he read recently of hospitals where "procedures for replacing broken light bulbs involve up to seventeen persons and twenty minutes of administrative time".

Of course, hospital life could come as a bit of a shock until you got used to it. According to Russell Cleaver, FAU came to stand for "faeces and urine"; it was a description that stuck. Of Brook Hospital Paul Fox writes: "I had never seen an adult naked, let alone bath, take them to the toilet, clean them up after, shave, wash hair and feed them. ....When I think about it now I am surprised how I coped. From 7 am to 8 am I was often the only person on a ward of 30 old men and a side ward of four ladies....on nights the same happened except when matron came round."

Ian Trott was an operating theatre orderly on the Thoracic Unit at Brook and writes: "The experience of greatest value was learnt while holding patients' hands during operations and investigations. The contacts made in these moments of major stress were to give me an insight which I might never otherwise have had." And Alan Quilley, in the same job at the same hospital some years later, remarks "I was certainly put off the idea of ever taking up smoking having seen the condition of some of the lungs which were removed – I usually had to carry them in a bowl over to the path.lab. I was present at one of the first open-heart operations carried out in Britain, when the patient on the table was surrounded by masses of ice to reduce the body temperature."

At Malvern too, chest surgery was frequent. This was a TB hospital, not as unusual in 1950s Britain as it would be today. As Tony Bristow writes: "Treatment was still a lengthy process offering not a complete cure but the slow creation of a condition where the disease was reasonably quiescent......Some patients were on medication, some had had surgery and some were committed to a long period of bed rest so that they could become sufficiently strong to have surgery."

At Malvern, as at many other hospitals, staffing had become a problem. John Hume writes: "There was full employment, but health service employees, especially unskilled ward orderlies, had low pay rates, and the only way they could earn a reasonable wage was by working a lot of overtime and unsocial hours – these being relatively better paid than nowadays. So instead of having a theoretical staffing level of an assistant nurse and an orderly per 20-bed ward, I well remember being in sole charge of three wards at night – and you can imagine how hectic that was in the morning."

John Hume also remembers having to "cough" patients after thoracic surgery, "holding their chests front and back and praying that their stitches would not pop open". That was on the post-operatic ward, but most wards held long-term patients on medication. Roger Bush noted that "some were very ill, though remaining cheerful and hopeful – for the first time I appreciated Thomas Mann's description of 'the hope of the phthisical'." But by 1955 Raymond Penrose could record that the rate of discharge had speeded up "as new drugs were coming out – PAS and terramycin". TB was an indiscriminate enemy and patients came from all walks of life. A celebrated patient on one ward was the radio actor Denis Folwell – Jack Archer in "The Archers", a role he played for many years despite having to attend St Wulstan's as an in-patient from time to time.

Perhaps because it was one of the larger hospital sections, with up to 12 members, St Wulstan's seems to have been well liked by most of those who served there. Jasper Kay says: "St Wulstan's taught me not to be afraid of hospitals, and how to play snooker!" And David Robson, who went on to a career in the Health Service, returned to work at the hospital during university summer vacations in 1956 and 1957, as did John Hume. The surroundings may have had something to do with it. Tony Bristow took part in the Malvern Beacon Race and the Worcester County championship, and records that "a year later, Martin Hyman joined the section and became a star in local cross-country events". (Russell Cleaver, who remembers going out on a training run with Martin when working for OCFR in London, later found that he had been running with Britain's representative in the 10,000 and 5000 metres at the Tokyo Olympics.) For Roger Bush night shifts meant that he was able to get to rehearsals for the first performance of Vaughan Williams's "Hodie" and other music at the Three Choirs Festival in Worcester in 1954. Others remember the poetry evenings at the home of Stan and Doris Salt and the gramophone record recitals in the flat belonging to Alice, the Lady Almoner. On the other hand, a later section member, Euan Pearson, who admits to being less happy with hospital sections because of "the petty snobbery (nurses and orderlies punished for fraternising out of hours)", says that he "positively loathed Malvern, despite the location".

The last hospital section to be established, in October 1955, was at Hackney in East London, where four members worked in the operating theatre, outpatients department and casualty. David Walker, who was an operating theatre orderly there in 1957, remembers "occasionally holding the limbs that the surgeon was amputating!". For Richard Jones, who was there in 1956, a training in chemistry combined with his experience at St Wulstans and Hackney, seeing "at first hand the practical benefits of chemotherapy", to reinforce his ambition to work in the field of medicine. He eventually he left FAUIS to take up a post at the Institute of Cancer Research. It is an appropriate postscript. As Richard writes of subsequent developments in his work there: it "is, indeed, remote from the humdrum routine of the work we did as hospital ward orderlies in our FAUIS days. And yet 'reverence for life' was implicit in the Service's purpose and activities. Maybe the unspoken assumptions had a greater influence than we and those around us were able to recognise at the time".

FORESTRY

In April 1950 Occasional Information was able to record a significant success: "Enquiries and negotiations have been made over several months about the possibility of establishing a permanent Forestry Section in England. At one time it was hoped that a group could work at a small forest near Basingstoke, but cuts in government expenditure resulted in the cancellation of the arrangement. In the Lake District and further north there are still opportunities open to us, and we intend to open a Section at Thornthwaite....". Andrew Long (Section Leader), Simon Cohen, Dennis Tomlin, John Donovan, Alan Lawrance and Donald White formed this first forestry section. In the event, work among the Norway and Sitka spruce around the Whinlatter pass – brashing, clearing drains in neglected forest, peeling saplings for pit props and fencing stakes – lasted just three months, but it was a start. The hostel accommodation was a wooden hut on the main road, two and a half miles walk from the working site, with primitive sanitary arrangements and no bath (there is a reference to members going down to Bassenthwaite for a dip). "The food was quite inadequate" writes Simon Cohen. "The same urn was used for tea and coffee which could not be distinguished from each other. We were given a packet of jam sandwiches for lunch which we usually ate on the way up to the forest and before even starting work... After supper each evening we tried not to think about food. A trip into Keswick by bicycle for fish and chips used as many calories as it provided." Indeed these conditions were behind the decision to transfer the section at the end of July to Kershopefoot on the Scottish Border. Members who served at this latter distant outpost over the years – it was regarded by many as a Siberian posting – will appreciate the irony. Strange too that members at Thornthwaite should have talked of "having overcome the language difficulties" there, when at Kershopefoot this was to be a renewed problem.

By September 1950 the new forestry section at Kershopefoot was finding its feet in sticky mud, with boots still wet from the day before. There were just three rainless days that summer. Nevertheless, those in charge of the work, mainly road building for the Forestry Commission's engineering branch, were satisfied with progress. As for the accommodation, Occasional Information reported: "The hostel is utilitarian, the location remote and the community small. Comforts are few and the use of leisure is a serious problem." Horst Diering, an associate member from East Germany who served there through the

1950/51 winter, puts it with a truly English measure of under-statement: "In Kershopefoot lebten wir recht einfach...". Others were less polite. Brian Geeson arrived there in January 1952, another severe winter: "Conditions were grim. We were housed in a large, gloomy Nissen hut, heated only by an inadequate, cen-trally placed coke stove. You sat near and scorched your face while your bum froze. Across the yard was an ablutions block, scarcely heated; in winter it was unthinkable to shave there. The bogs – for toilets they never were – were in a ramshackle lean-to, near the burn. Their contents were archaeological. The food was utterly wretched, with either sago or rice pudding for afters every night." But he stuck with it until the summer when the camp was winding down, the Nissen huts closed and better accommodation available, and in the end left it with regret: "It was entirely unex-pected that this Siberia should become such a delightful place".

Though around that time the section shrunk to a mere hand-ful, Kershopefoot was a long-standing commitment and kept going through 1953. Roger Bland found them still road building the following winter: "Lorry loads of quarry stone and rubble were reversed and off-loaded onto a thick mattress of brashings, and we set to work with sledge-hammers on the larger boulders and shovels on the rest." He noticed the importance of draining: "Ditches were cut on either side of the road using a unique trian-gular shaped cutting tool (a rutter) and smooth run-off for water was created using a long, narrow 'bottoming' shovel". When Ian Trott was there a lack of gloves caused a minor incident: the win-ter handling of stones became impossible, the Unit had no money for gloves, the Forestry Commission expected workers to supply their own and refused to find alternative work for the section, and a withdrawal of labour was only prevented by a trip to Carlisle where members bought gloves at their own expense.

As forestry sections went, Kershopefoot was the most like an overseas assignment. Brian Geeson noted, the "local men were a rough, foul-mouthed lot who held us in open contempt". For Roger Bush the natives at the camp "seemed strange to us Southrons, men and women hairy alike as protection against the cold, thick of accent, and mostly smokers from an early age. Tobacco wasn't cheap, even then, and one would find small toddlers begging for cigarette ends. Some of the foresters smoked revolting pine-needle herbal mixtures...". Even so, he "learned to pronounce the name of the local 'ville lumière', Hawick". By his account "Scottish nationalism was beginning to take root on the other side of the Kershope Burn. It was said that if you could see a light burning in the derelict hut on Tinnis Hill, the more extreme elements were meeting that night. The rest of England seemed a long way away, beyond the afforested ridges and the mysterious missile-testing area of Spadeadam Waste...".

In the Spring of 1951 a new commitment was negotiated with the Forestry Commission – felling and thinning in forest near Crawley – and a withdrawal from Kershopefoot was considered. But against the isolation and cost of transporting members to the Borders had to be set the higher cost of living in the South East: food and accommodation at Crawley's Tilgate Hostel cost 45 shillings a week for each member, compared with 35 shillings at Kershopefoot. In the end, Kershope's road building continued alongside the more conventional forestry work in Sussex.

"We arranged with the Forester", writes Ray Ferris, the first Section Leader at Crawley, "to produce an agreed quota every day, rather than just to work hours. This was to provide motivation and create long breaks by working harder. It worked well, and we always produced well over quota, although working for much less of the day. The Forester wrote 'We are surprised at the staggering example set by your men to our local workers. We would like to hire as many as you can spare'. The thoughts of the "local workers" are unrecorded.

Southwater, near Horsham, became the home of the new forestry section in November 1951. A hostel built ten years earlier for agricultural workers was made available by the Forestry Commission, with accommodation for about twenty and some land for a kitchen garden. Not as idyllic as it sounds, though. David Gray was Section Leader there at the start of 1952, in charge of a mixed group which included a number of associate members from Germany. "I don't think we did much more internationally than to 'get along socially', with good humour, living in cold damp huts and working in cold wet woodlands. We were selectively felling and clearing trees and undergrowth in birch heathland, preparatory to replanting with straight rows of conifers. With hindsight, as a conservationist, I grieve over this conversion of broadleaved heathland into conifer farming. But it was 'manly work', swinging an axe in the snowy woods...". The following year another Section Leader, Tony Bristow, remembers "the summer task was to spend most of the time bent half double and moving slowly forwards along the rows, cutting down the weeds and looking anxiously for the next sapling ahead. A spruce bifurcates if you cut the top off, and double pit-props or telephone poles are not in great demand." Howard Brunton also writes of "trying to persuade a bunch of Brits, Germans and an Israeli not to lop the tops off too many of the young pine trees we were supposed to be weeding". Richard Errington went to Southwater with John Gaskin, another Section Leader there and "a man who felt a certain amount of military discipline would not come amiss – I don't think we ever paraded formally but I'm sure he would have fully endorsed the idea". According to Ray Ferris, Gaskin set a fine example and a blistering pace – he would plant 1200 trees a day – "and, strive as we might, none of us could come within a hundred of him".

According to John Hume, at Southwater in 1954, the Head Forester there (Mr Aubery) "did not have a very high opinion of the pink soft-handed new members of FAUIS – we had to earn his grudging approval by learning quickly and working hard". Without that approval he "regarded the 18-year old time rate of £2.5.0 a week as somewhat generous".

Of the Southwater hostel Richard Jones remembers: "beside the all-pervading night cold, there was the recalcitrant stove which had to be coaxed into action before we could roast the Sunday joint". That stove; nearly three years earlier Michael Pittard was sent from Melksham to put in a kitchen at the hostel. "The building had a centrally placed door with a baffle wall a yard or so inside to frustrate the worst of the draught. Through this door we wished to introduce a second-hand ESSE cooker without dismantling it. This was achieved by chipping away at the base of the wall until it was detached from the floor and placing rollers underneath it and moving it to one side to be replaced once the cooker was safely inside."

Was it PWS, Michael asks, rather unkindly, which had the motto "give us the job and we will finish the tools"? (The cooker returned in a similar way to Lavender Farm when Southwater closed in 1956.)

The last of the forestry sections started up in October 1955 at Shoreham in the Sevenoaks area of Kent, where a semi-detached cottage was leased from the Forestry Commission as a hostel. Within a year it had taken over from Southwater. For Paul Fox the work consisted of "cutting down great bramble bushes while looking for six-inch-high conifer trees. By the end of the day I thought I was a slave on a sugar plantation."

And Ian Ricketts remembers in particular six acres of Ide Hill, cleared, fenced and planted to completion: "It was one of those rare occasions when the Commission had intelligence enough, or by chance allowed, a sense of being identified with a piece of land long enough to care about it, and all of us did in our own way. It is still a kind of metaphor."

Forestry was a useful earner and undoubtedly did much for the health of IS members. "I did not know what it all had to do with pacifism, but the work was satisfying and there was camaraderie in the hostel at the end of a hard day" David Maxwell reflects. The forester's calling intrigued Keith Tyler –"planting thousands of trees whose maturity one would never see". But Alan Quilley went back to look at the Ide Hill trees in 1985 and found the site unrecognisable, the trees had grown so tall. And Jasper Kay was able to point out to his disbelieving offspring the trees that daddy had planted at Southwater.

By 1957 the reduction in Unit numbers meant that forestry had to give way to hospital and overseas work; Shoreham closed down at the end of May and with it this chapter of IS activity.

CHAPTER 8

Floods, earthquakes and political uprisings

FIRST CAME THE floods. Under a full moon, the conjunc-
tion of high spring tides and hurricane force winds at the
start of February 1953 brought disastrous flooding to the North
Sea coasts of East Anglia and of the Netherlands. Sea defences
were smashed, thousands of acres were under water, people were
drowned, whole herds of livestock perished, villages were cut off
by sea water. In Holland it was the worst flooding for over five
centuries. Almost the entire province of Zeeland was inundated,
as well as huge areas of North Brabant and South Holland; 2000
people lost their lives and many thousands more their homes.

David Fairbanks was working at Southwater when the FAUIS
was asked for help by a local Friend, Harold Thomas (ex-FAU
1914-18), owner of a building used as a community centre and a
Meeting House on Canvey Island. Here the dykes, originally
built by the Dutch centuries earlier, had been breached in many
places, and much of the island was under water. As a native of
Westcliff-on-Sea, and having himself previously lived on Canvey,
David was a natural choice to join a small section under Colin
Sorensen. "We started work ....by giving out clothing to flood victims and dyke workers. Later, when the floods subsided, small
teams of two to four members would clean out houses or, in
many cases, poor quality bungalows. These dwellings, mostly
located in unmade roads, had been erected as holiday homes
before the war, often just standing on four bricks. Salt water and

mud played havoc with the wooden structures and house contents..... One bungalow had been transported by the flood and left in the next road." After the main work of taking everything out, washing down the floors and wall and cleaning up whatever could be salvaged, the RAF were invited to bring along their electric dryers to dry out the building – a nice late example of co-operation with the Armed Services.

Though the section never rose above twelve in number, it had the use of two vehicles, a Jeep and a Ford Utility, and later an Austin truck and a Ford 3-ton lorry, all useful in transporting food and clothing. Bryan Reed, who took over as Section Leader from Colin Sorensen and stayed until the end of April, wrote: "The days of Operation Canute passed: the desperate sandbagging of the wall, the searching in rowing boats, the uncertain waiting for the next high tide.... Transport became the very mainspring of relief work.... The humping of waterlogged carpets and laundry, because the roads were too bad for a vehicle, was but one of the troubles....". Even tractors sometimes got stuck in the sinking mud, but "in an emergency we were frequently approached to provide the 'mules'".

Zeeland is the part of the Netherlands that pushes out into the sea around the Scheldt and Maas estuaries – literally the land of the sea, which flooded in looking to reclaim it. The Dutch are used to fighting the sea, and already by April 1953, when the first FAUIS teams arrived there, under Alan Fincham, who had worked on Canvey, parts of the province had been cleared of water. But that was only the beginning of the task; what was left was a wilderness of mud and silt, half-burying the damaged houses. Christopher Levenson described it dramatically in a leaflet published not much later: "Mussels and sea pox cluster on the sides of broken walls, and the only green comes not from grass but from seaweed. Dark, stinking cellars are studded with starfish and every stone upturned disturbs a nest of crabs. Each morning the dull light on the desert sand appears like frost ..... perpetual winter grips the besieged land. Normal harvests are at least six years off, and many people say crops will not grow again in this polder."

Holland, 1954: cleaning a mud-soaked wall, Nieuwekerk, Schouwen-Duiveland.
(PHOTO: JACK SKEEL)

Holland, 1953-4: picking over the rubble after disastrous floods.
(PHOTO: JACK SKEEL)

With Alan were David Fairbanks and Michael Reynolds, also with Canvey experience. The Coordinatie Commissie Hulpwerk (CCH) had been set up in Amsterdam to harness the efforts of voluntary and other organisations; the FAUIS team was sent first to Oude Tonge on Overflakke and then on to Schouwen Duiveland, part of Zeeland. "It was not until we reached the south side of Rotterdam that signs of flooding began to appear: damaged roads, muddy fields, sandbags and a general air of untidiness so foreign to Holland..... In many places the road and dyke had been torn away and the car had to bump over sand and metal sheets strewn along the way. Large quantities of timber, fencing posts, furniture, trees and, above all, onions littered the area – Zeeland is an onion-growing area." In Oude Tonge, where out of 886 houses only 51 had received no damage at all and 168 had been totally destroyed, the work was mainly demolition of houses and farm buildings that were in a dangerously precarious state.

At the new CCH camp in Dreischor on Schouwen Duiveland, David Fairbanks recounts a still more grim experience: "One day in early June, the Burgemeester of Dreischor asked for volunteers to assemble outside the church to spend the day searching for three villagers missing since the flood. ....All day we combed empty houses, gardens, hedgerows, fields and sheds. At about 6 pm I was one of four CCH members prodding a canal when a body was found. It took hours to drain off this section of the canal .... The other two people were never found."

Unit sections also worked at Bruinisse and Sir Jansland, two other villages, up to seven members at any one time, but by late summer large numbers of student work camp volunteers were available and it seemed sensible to withdraw temporarily. Later, in November 1953, two three-man sections returned to Schouwen Duiveland, and work continued at Ouwekerk and Nieuwekerk throughout a hard winter and into next spring.

At Ouwekerk, close to the sea dyke, giant waves had destroyed many of the houses. David Fairbanks, on his second visit to the area, was able to watch the last of the sea defences – giant, concrete caissons – being towed into place. A dyke builder explained to him how draining was organised: work starts wherever the flood has penetrated furthest, and water is pumped from polder to polder until it can at last be pumped back over the sea dyke. A visitor to the area these days will find it changed by the huge Delta project, closing the south-west sea arms with dykes carrying modern highways.

In May 1954 the CCH disbanded and handed over further work to government control. But that was not quite the end of work in Holland. In June 1955 ten members went to St Maartensdijk in Zeeland to help in putting up a prefabricated day nursery given by the Save the Children Fund of Sweden. Roger Bland, the Section Leader, wrote, shortly after their arrival: "We are the attraction of the village at the moment, the latest manifestation being a crowd of youngsters outside the window being entertained by David Robson and others with songs and music....". Obviously David put down his guitar once work started. The building, put up under the direction of Axel Huisberg, an architect from Stockholm, was opened only four months after the foundations were laid, and the section left at the end of November.

EARTHQUAKES IN GREECE

In less than a minute, on 12 August 1953, a major earthquake destroyed practically every home on the Ionian islands of Ithaca, Kephalonia and Zakynthos. Four hundred people were killed and over 100,000 made homeless. News of the disaster was prominent in British newspapers and on the radio; it was the second natural catastrophe of the year, but it aroused almost as big a public response as the earlier floods. The Royal Navy had been quickly on the scene, with other foreign navies in the Mediterranean, helping to provide emergency shelter and stores. It was clear, however, that a huge long-term building programme was needed.

The Greek Earthquake Appeal in London was chaired by the Rt. Hon. Philip Noel-Baker MP, a veteran of the First World War FAU. Through his good offices, FAUIS became affiliated to the Greek Red Cross and was accepted for help in the work of

*Greece, 1954: basic work on
foundations for a hospital.*
(PHOTO: JACK SKEEL)

Greece, 1954: unloading hospital supplies at Argostoli, Kephalonia.
(PHOTO: JACK SKEEL)

reconstruction. After some delays, during which several members were sent on an intensive course in the use of Dexion slotted-angle construction, the first team left for Athens in January 1954.

The early plans by the Greek Red Cross included five 16-bed hospitals. As in Holland, Sweden was prominent in supplying prefabricated buildings. Sten Dahlstrom was already on Kephalonia, at Argostoli, where relief supplies were warehoused, but his blue-prints were in English, which he read with difficulty. Although our team had no Swedish and neither they nor Sten spoke Greek, their assistance was welcome, and things worked out well enough for hospital buildings to be completed at Lixouri on Kephalonia and Vathi on Ithaca by the end of May. Shortly afterwards the Red Cross withdrew from the islands and FAUIS work had to be scaled down, but two members continued to work with Sten Dahlstrom on a third hospital at Mitica, on the Greek mainland but close to Levkas and other islands, and a fourth at Sami on Kephalonia.

In October a further four members went out to Metaxata, on Kephalonia, to help in putting up a school building, given by the Earthquake Appeal in Scotland and prefabricated in aluminium by the Bristol Aeroplane Company's Housing Division. Organising any building programme in the islands had always been difficult, and by now FAUIS was the only foreign organisation working there. Prospects for further work did not look good, and three members went instead to Panayitsa, near Salonika, to help with preparations for a distribution of food and clothing from the USA in poverty-stricken Thessaly. In fact the largest and most adventurous project was yet to come. This was to be an orphanage on Zakynthos, an Arcon building given by the Bible Lands Missions Aid Society and originally to have been built by the Greek army. Despite illness among the section and political troubles in Greece, work on it was completed and it was opened in February 1956 by Lady Peake, wife of the British Ambassador.

That is no more than a brief account of the Unit's involvement in earthquake and other work in Greece. Just as that country occupies an important place in the history of the World War Two FAU, so it does with the FAUIS. Work there brought its members into contact with a way of life so different from that of northern Europe, it was more identifiable with end products – hospitals, a school and an orphanage, and it was the most ambitious programme in terms of travel and expense. The following extracts from reports and accounts written both at the time and later give something of the atmosphere of a now not-so-far-off place at a time when it seemed a great deal more distant.

Robert Stokes's first impressions, Spring 1954: "There are very few workmen on the islands. Most of those working with us have come from the mainland. They seem to return to the islands to marry and retire.... By our standards they seem poor, and there is a real class structure. The carpenter is definitely distinct from the labourer. Lorry drivers are a select group. Anyone who can manage to walk around with an umbrella does so, foreman-like." And on the Greek Red Cross: "We have an enormous admiration for the work of the Sisters of the Greek Red Cross, especially in the smaller centres like Lixouri and Ithaca. They work very hard looking after the small hospitals and medical rooms – distributing food and clothing and being a help to everyone." He was privileged to attend a baptism in a small one-roomed house in Lixouri: "Christenings in any land are usually times of rejoicing, but in this case there was a note of pathos running through the whole ceremony. The child's father was dead – killed by the earthquake. The mother was expecting the child at the time."

From a report by the distribution team in mainland Greece: "Our job divided itself into two instalments: firstly a clothing distribution in Macedonia to about a thousand families, and secondly the main work in Thessaly, where over four thousand families are to be helped with gifts of both food and clothing. In the earthquake area of Thessaly there are two centres, and here we are giving to families officially classed as below the poverty line. 'Poverty' in this case means an income of less than ten cents a head per day – enough to buy two cups of coffee in a Greek coffee-shop. (There are more coffee-shops per square inch in Greece than in any other country in the world..)... Through the Bishop of Karditsa our attention was drawn to certain destitute mountain villages, who have not been lucky enough to have an earthquake, and hence have received little help from abroad. Our distribution to some of these communities will take place in a monastery high up in the hills, to which villagers are to come on foot or by donkey and mule." Bill Roff wrote: "The distribution in Pharsala, despite politics and the giving of favours, which stopped work for a day, has proceeded smoothly and is now completed. The army, having brought three lorry loads to Pharsala, will take four to Karditsa tomorrow. It seems strange that the army should be our best friends. They know our convictions, but it does not affect their generosity... Tom Braun is at Larisa making sure that the army send the right bales, and will go... to Karditsa, to make arrangements with the Bishop and others with him... When we have served Karditsa's thousand-odd families and the 130 of a village, we shall be living in a monastery to give food to 2,000 families."

And in Macedonia: "The civil war that ended only five years ago was at its worst in this frontier area, and it is not only the destroyed houses that testify to this terrible time. We found ourselves distributing to an astonishingly large proportion of widows." To an astonishing proportion of large widows too, apparently. Among the first words of Greek the team learned were "too tight" as "Greek women, we found, vary considerably in girth from their American benefactresses. Pyjamas and underwear seemed to many people to be unknown quantities.." One of the team remembers "the self-respecting refugee family, typical, I think, of many of those we helped, who invited me into their clean and completely bare one-roomed dwelling, offered me a cup of coffee and asked me everything about myself. Wasn't it very sad for me to be working so far from home? How did we all manage without our mothers to take care of us? The lady of the house was all sympathy. 'Please give me your address,' she said, 'so that I can knit some socks and send them to you. I feel you boys need our help.'"

On the political troubles, here is Tony Bristow, on a visit to Athens to find exterior paint for the orphanage on Zakynthos:

"When I left Zakynthos last Friday all was calm, but I walked into the excitement in Athens, hearing of Makarios's deportation in Piraeus and finding myself on the outskirts of a demonstration..... There were squads of police on every corner and over a hundred armed soldiers surrounded the British Embassy. I was actually inside at midday and met Sir Charles Peake whose recall seemed probable at the time; it was a strange feeling for a pacifist to be under armed protection..".

And lastly an apt illustration of just one of the negotiating problems that regularly beset Tony Bristow and other Section Leaders in the Ionian Islands – the story of the flagpole:

"Mr Malafouris said that ODAZ (the Public Welfare Organisation of Zakynthos) would like a flagpole fitted and would pay for it, but would I arrange with a blacksmith for the fittings and with the carpenter for the pole. The blacksmith was with us for another task, and for an hour I discussed with him the fittings necessary in relation to the skeleton of the building. When I saw the carpenter he said he could not buy such wood, could I get it from the government store? I went to Mr Malafouris to know whether ODAZ wished me to make this request and subsequently visited the deputy chief engineer three times before I found him (in). He said there was no suitable wood in the stores; I must have Dexion. I saw Mr Malafouris; he said Dexion would be all right. Then I saw the carpenter and told him that I could not get wood, whereupon he said there was wood in the shops but it was expensive. Once again to Mr Malafouris who said he would rather take Dexion than buy wood, but could I enquire for wood at the store. I visited the store and was shown suitable wood and I then saw the carpenter again who confirmed that this wood was satisfactory. Off to the deputy chief engineer again who now confessed he had orders not to sanction wood for such jobs, but he sent me to the Chief Engineer, who as Director of the Stores could sanction it. The Chief Engineer said he would love to give me wood but there was none so (a) I had not seen it, (b) I could not have it. He sent for a clerk who studied a catalogue and confirmed that the wood I had seen did not exist. I reported to the carpenter and eventually Mr Malafouris, and meanwhile collected the Dexion. It transpired that there was an error on the form which said 8 pieces, 24 metres. Each piece is in fact 3.048 metres but this discrepancy was cleared up after a telephone call to the aforementioned clerk. By this time the blacksmith was ill and so I had to arrange with another and for an hour I discussed the fittings necessary ..... but this is where we came in."

THE HUNGARIAN UPRISING

By the summer of 1956 work in the Ionian Islands was drawing to a close. Membership of the Unit was reducing in the wake of uncertainty about the future of National Service. There was uncertainty too about exactly what a smaller Unit could offer. Events in October changed all that; by the end of the year resources of manpower and vehicles were stretched to the limit. Twenty members out of the total of 67 were directly engaged in Hungarian relief work, either in Austria or with the British Council for Aid to Refugees in Britain.

On the first day of November, Chris Driver set out for Budapest with six parcels of drugs and antibiotics, purchased with money raised at a public meeting a few days earlier and given to the FAU to use as best it could. By the time he reached Vienna the Austro-Hungarian border had been firmly sealed, but it was found possible to get the drugs onto a barge down the Danube consigned to a Budapest hospital. If traffic into Hungary was impossible, it was clear at once that there was going to be a growing refugee problem. South of Vienna up to 5000 a night were pouring over the frontier. A team of American and British Friends from the Quakerhaus in Vienna had gone out to the barracks at Traiskirchen where refugees were being received, and they were reinforced by an FAUIS section which built up to 15 in number. The use of Traiskirchen finished early in 1957, but the section, accommodated in the Quakerhaus, still had plenty of work. Bales of clothing delivered by rail were taken to a deserted factory at Atzgersdorf on the outskirts of Vienna, where they were sorted by a group of Hungarian refugees working under FAUIS direction. Communication with them was in German – one of their number spoke German as did Peter Pilkington and several of the FAUIS members.

As the 1957 Report put it the Unit was concerned at nearly all the points in the chain that carried a garment from a hook in somebody's wardrobe to the back of a refugee in a camp in

Austria. At OCFR warehouses in London members sorted and baled clothing, FAU vehicles took bales out across Europe, or collected them from airport or railhead in Austria, and the section at Traiskirchen delivered sorted articles on the camp sites. Vehicles were important throughout the whole Hungarian relief operation.

Pat Oakley was a former PWS member working in Bristol as a trainee probation officer when he heard that the FAUIS needed a driver to take a converted Leyland bus out to Vienna. His Home Office employers accorded him leave, and he reported to Lavender Farm to collect the vehicle. As he told Jack Norton years later: "I complained to some idiot, possibly you, that there was no jack and was told with great glee that I wouldn't need one as there was no spare wheel anyway....". Despite a puncture and, after loading up with two tons of chocolate and bales of clothing, breaking a rear spring when they had got no further than Vauxhall, he and his co-drivers drove it to Vienna, non-stop by turns at a regulated thirty miles an hour.

Keith Tyler writes of the "huge barracks at Traiskirchen, recently plundered of every unscrewable item by the retiring Russians, and, as a processing transit camp, uncomfortably like an allied concentration camp...". Though Pat Oakley had doubts about how the bus would be maintained in Austria, he remembers it being used to transport personnel "for which it was very effective, because having no seats you could take 50 or 60 people standing up". Less so was the chocolate: an experienced relief worker told him that people who had been underfed were prone to develop diarrhoea if they were given chocolate and ate too much of it.

Driving the bus was a job that later fell to David Correa Hunt, an associate member who was a professionally licensed PSV driver. He recalls being sent on a special mission to Andau, between the Neusiedlersee and the frontier, where there was a shelter run by Save the Children fund. "The Hungarian escape route involved long wading through the icy marshes. Sound carries far over that flat expanse, and silence was essential to avoid alerting the then rather widely spaced frontier posts. An infant's cry in the night would be sure to draw the searchlight's beam – and worse. It was therefore vital to the success of their escape that fleeing families should sedate their very young ones,and this was often done unscientifically with overdoses of aspirin, with the result that many couples succeeded in getting across to Freedom only to find their babes dying in their arms.." He writes of the "wonderful SCF nurse, operating the shelter single-handed" whose task it was "to revive the comatose infants on their arrival: literally to save the children".

Reports of those babies evidently reached the American press, for John Lawson writes: "They sent out 200 tons of baby food in small bottles; we couldn't get rid of the stuff". From England came evening dress and tails with the clothes: "What do we do with that? We fitted out Budapest musicians for the Vienna Philharmonic orchestra. Also the bass singer for the Budapest Opera gave us a private audience – he was fantastic."

The trucking of supplies using Unit vehicles continued well into 1957, and later in that year shipments were taken as far as Belgrade and Zagreb to cater for Hungarian refugees in Yugoslav camps. A section of four transferred to live in Lager Wegscheid, a refugee camp outside Linz, in March to help with the building of a small estate of prefabricated timber houses for families living in the overcrowded camp. "Generally speaking" says John Lawson "Austria got the rump end of it all. The healthy, young and bright refugees were snapped up by the USA, Canada and Australia. Austria was left with the criminals, prostitutes, and street cleaners, who can survive under most political dynasties". A harsh verdict – as Brian King points out "most refugees stuck in Austria were decent folk but less skilled and older or, because of their experiences, old before their time". Brian was sent to join a group of four members at Windischgarten, in the mountains, to help erect a prefabricated annexe to a Swedish Mission's Mutterheim, and then went to Lager Wegscheid, to help the Mission with transport and with building work. Here his job was not only to follow up the Mission's list of refugees who needed assistance with self-help building schemes, but also to build up the section, finding work opportunities through interviewing refugees and assessing their needs and taking on more FAU members – as

FAU vehicles at a checkpoint on the Trieste-Vienna run, 1957.
(PHOTO: JOHN PREVETT)

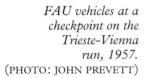

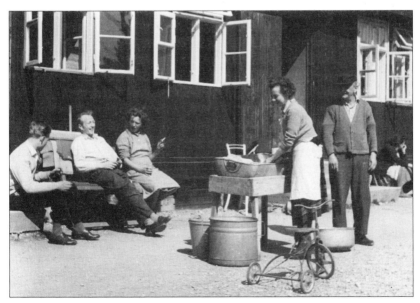

Austria, 1957: a typical refugee-camp scene, Lager Wegscheid, Linz.
(PHOTO: PAUL FOX)

many as possible. Among the refugees who had embarked on self-help building were some who had taken Austrian nationality, thus losing their refugee status and aid. Often their health and income did not match their ambitions to build their own houses. Members of the section had to develop building skills – plastering, carpentry and floor laying – in addition to labouring work. As well as placing various unemployed refugees in their building and transport work teams, they found themselves acting as organisers for some 50 United Nations Association volunteers from a summer work camp. They also entered fully into the fellowship of the camp, to the extent of suffering an 11-2 defeat at football in a game with a Hungarian eleven.

Standards in Austria appear to have been better than those at Valka Camp, near Nuremburg, the only reception-transit camp in Germany. Peter Leeming, who went there with a small section assisting the FSC/AFSC 'Employment Project' in finding temporary or permanent jobs and resettlement for non-German refugees applying for asylum in the Federal Republic, writes: "Valka was a grim place, looking like a concentration camp, surrounded by barbed wire. The original intention was to keep the refugees locked up, partly because of fear of it becoming a route for easy infiltration by spies.... The UNHCR intervened to keep the gate open, but the Bavarian government refused to allow the inmates to do any kind of work in the area. We negotiated – or rather FSC did – the solution that work could be found in another state of Germany provided the refugees made every effort to emigrate to USA, Australia etc. Since they mostly proved to be such excellent workers and contributed to the German economy, many of them settled in Germany and the condition was quietly forgotten!". The job here was rather different from those at Austrian and other sections – interviewing refugees and negotiating with the camp authorities for them to be sent for interview and work in Stuttgart or Cologne where there were FSC/AFSC links with employment offices. It demanded a high level of fluency in German as well as typing and office skills, and above all an ability to liaise with Bavarian officialdom – something that could only be learnt 'on the job'.

Resettlement was also providing work for the Unit at home. Soon after the first group of members had gone out to Vienna, the first Hungarian refugees began to arrive in England. The work of the British Council for Aid to Refugees was supported by a team of three, with three vehicles, and a fourth in London, ferrying interpreters to Blackbushe airport – the main point of entry – and refugees to transit hostels in Hampshire and Essex. Petrol rationing made all transport difficult at this time, and the FAUIS contribution was especially welcome.

Later the vehicles and their drivers were transferred to Hednesford, Staffordshire, where a camp for 5000 was being set up. Until the closing of this camp in September 1957, the FAUIS was responsible for ambulance, station wagon, fire engine and school bus transport, and, once it became clear that it would be more than a short-term transit camp, two members co-operated with Hungarian teachers in starting a school which was later recognised and paid for by the local education authority. David Walker remembers "taking refugees to be interviewed for jobs, moving them to new lives in Birmingham, Coventry, Wolverhampton, and even, on one occasion, to church to be married. All this in the good old Bedford trucks!". In 1996 he went back to Hednesford camp: "All the buildings have gone, and there are trees 30 feet high where the transport office used to be".

This body of refugee work was the last major project of the FAUIS. By the end of 1958, when there were only 19 members left, the only overseas sections were at Linz and Nuremburg, and these too closed in 1959.

CHAPTER 9

Life at headquarters 1951-59

SHAW HILL LIES about a mile and a half from the market town of Melksham in Wiltshire, on the road to Bath. In the 1940s it became the home of Beltane, a progressive school moved there from south-west London. Jack Norton, when he joined the infant International Service as General Secretary in August 1950, had been bursar and joint principal at Beltane. As director and secretary of the limited company that ran the school he took control of it after the decision by its founders, the Tomlinsons, to retire.

Although Jack joined the HQ staff at Petersfield, his connection with Beltane remained a strong one. A small section, just two members, went there to do plumbing and general maintenance work, and were later joined by two more on cooking duties. These were followed in February 1951 by a "probationers' course", held in some semi-derelict buildings on the Beltane campus, and by April there were four "HQ constructional workers" busy turning this surplus accommodation into a new HQ for the International Service.

Traffic between Petersfield and Melksham continued through the summer, but in October Dunannie was vacated. Lavender Farm, the collective name for the Beltane outbuildings, became the new home of the FAUIS. The school itself was moved to High Canons in Hertfordshire, but Jack Norton had retained the farm and four acres of land, including the cottage where he, his wife and son were living.

Lavender Farm, Melksham, 1956.
(PHOTO: JOHN PREVETT)

There was more in the move of headquarters than a change of accommodation. If the Unit was to survive, there had also to be a change of direction. Subscription income had been falling, and although membership was increasing and with it the earning capacity through paid employment, there was a need to cut costs through a headquarters establishment that was simpler and cheaper to run and that offered more scope for home industry. Pig keeping, started at Petersfield, was to be expanded and joined by poultry keeping. There was to be more emphasis on self-sufficiency, and this too would provide on-the-spot labouring opportunities, without the need to travel to and from a place of work – something that had been disruptive to the social life of the Petersfield community.

For the next five and a half years Melksham was the FAUIS headquarters.

The Lavender Farm site comprised a frontage on the Shaw Hill road, single-storey buildings surrounding a courtyard, the General Secretary's cottage and attached walled garden, and various outbuildings. In September 1951 Brian Geeson found it a bit Spartan after the amenities of an Oxford college, "more like a Youth Hostel of the most primitive kind. The move from the old HQ at Petersfield was not complete, and several rooms were unusable... we were assured that life would improve." At that stage the communal rooms were complete and, as Occasional Information put it "ready to incite the criticism of members and visitors on colours, workmanship and functional arrangement. The colour scheme of the main block is suited to Festival Year, and members who have worked there can rightly feel that their meagre materials have been used almost as effectively as those at South Bank.....The office block will be much less lively in decoration...". Brian remembers painting an office ceiling jet black – but perhaps that was the only paint left over. By December the pig parlours were almost complete, capacious ones able to take a sow and litter. Colin Henderson, Unit Cashier at the time, had to be "careful to distinguish between our subscriptions to the SPCK and the SPKC (The Society for the Propagation of Christian Knowledge and the Small Pig Keepers Council)".

The garden was in a very presentable condition, trees had been pruned and the last quarter of an acre was being dug over. Between them the two walled gardens and the greenhouse were meant to supply the needs of the HQ kitchen and to bring in money by selling the surplus in Melksham – in 1952 to a cafe and a local greengrocer. Negotiating prices, and getting fruit and vegetables picked in time to meet their needs, were both tricky problems for the gardener and the Quartermaster.

Early in the following year Colin Reed contributed to the Circular Letter which enabled members to write about their own sections and work to the Unit as a whole: "A few members have tried to send out something out to sections about the life here at Headquarters but as yet no one has been able to write about it satisfactorily and I do not propose to try now. The work here is varied with everyone doing something different and no two members would write alike about it." Quite so. It is probably best to consider life at HQ under the headings of the activities that seem to have been most important to members.

Cooks and cooking

Most people did a turn in the kitchen and the kitchen did some to a turn. Brian Geeson was given the post of Cook Number Three, but soon won promotion and struggled with a fortnightly cycle of menus under the eagle eye of Quartermaster Tom Campbell, anxious to stretch stocks as far possible. A year later, when he returned to Lavender Farm on a fleeting visit, he found only two cooks "pigging it alone in solitary splendour in the scullery". Why, he asked them, were they eating there and not in the Dining Room? "Because it's safer" they replied, and he felt that he understood.

Richard Errington learned cooking with David Taylor, who at least had some training as a caterer, but still remembers "an injudicious purchase of coffee beans (raw)" and the soup "always on the boil to absorb leftovers". For Roger Bush, the best cook was John Geale "who worked wonders with the materials available producing what I termed at the time 'real Geale meal appeal'". And Christopher Driver's time as cook elevated the quality of HQ menus to rare heights. "Those of us who assisted him learned all manner of skills" says Nick Evens. Others will remember that the kitchen contained a collection of vegetable colourings, which would be used by less skilled cooks to give novelty to pedestrian offerings, a crimson rice pudding perhaps, or green gravy. If one item of diet stands out it is probably peanut butter, which would arrive in industrial-size drums.

Training camps

Some training in cooking was regarded as part of the training camp curriculum. Since these camps were mostly run by former members of the Unit, they reflected these members' own training, but even so were somewhat more relaxed affairs than those at Petersfield. New recruits started their probationary period with a programme that included first aid and elementary hospital nursing techniques, accounting, some light drill, games and sports, long runs and route marches, gardening skills, concreting, building methods and some languages. Then there were the initiative tests, thought by some to be a device of Jack Norton's for researching new enterprises, but often making new entrants think about some of the problems they might face in the course of their service. Thus one might be asked to set up a soup kitchen to serve sixty to seventy people, another to work out the economics of a pig farm. Richard Jones was asked to descend on Bristol with the job of organising accommodation, clothing and employment for "a few score phantom refugees" but found the social services, and residents, full of goodwill when the mission was explained to them. In 1955 new recruits also cut their teeth on building work for something more real – a three-pump Esso petrol station at Lavender Farm.

House and garden

Michael Pittard, with a farming background, spent sixteen months as pig and poultry keeper and gardener at Melksham. "I recall the sow with one blue and one brown eye who would release herself from her sty and proceed via the main road to the yard to rummage in the kitchen waste bins....There were the rat hunts after dark armed with kitchen mops and battens, or better still hockey sticks, directed at the rats which visited the poultry arks on the green...". Richard Brown wrote about the building of those arks: "It was quite an interesting job but exasperating at times because it ate wood and all of ours is secondhand and the wrong lengths, thicknesses and widths. Most of the materials except paint are secondhand and it all adds to the difficulties...". Others at that time were busy building the pig sties: "The chap in charge is someone from Sidcot who trained as an architect" (David Butler, who went on to design Quaker meeting houses).

Before going to Greece, Bob Stokes was the HQ gardener for a year. His memories include "the lush green growth of the cucumber plants in the greenhouse, watered from the deep tank made of slate slabs; picking Brussels sprouts with frost on them; helping to get all the pigs to the slaughterhouse when swine fever

had been diagnosed; the apple trees in full blossom and scent...".
Other, more exotic crops were grown: there is a mention of
tobacco being harvested – but not cannabis.

Roger Baker remembers "the difficulties of marketing crisp
but brown-edged lettuce". And Roger Bush remembers "wrapping hundreds of apples from the specimen trees in the walled
garden, wrapping them for some reason in pages from a book of
prints of Audubon birds and antique ballet costumes. These
must have come as part of a sale lot, the source of many things at
Lavender Farm. I can picture now two dozen lavatory seats being
carried together on a pole to one of the outbuildings; the twenty-
fifth had gone to replace a broken seat somewhere on the
premises." Perhaps, though Michael Pittard describes "some
rather superior mahogany jobs" that ended up "framing portraits
of Gladstone and Keir Hardie and hanging in the dining hall".

Unit members who worked longer at Lavender Farm, like
John Veit Wilson, "eventually graduated from the dormitories for
the transients to small bedrooms to themselves behind the
kitchen. Small is the only word; my bed had only two legs
because it had to rest on the ledge which ran along the wall under
the windows, and sometimes fell off them."

The vehicles

The move to Lavender Farm and the development of workshops there undoubtedly prolonged the life of several historic
FAU vehicles, which were practically falling to pieces. They were
rebuilt and maintained so successfully that veterans like the ex-
WD Bedford trucks (HGH – vehicles were usually known by
their registration letters) were able to take members, stores and
supplies across Europe five years later, following the Hungarian
crisis. Though they could on occasion convey members and
stores to and from sections, for much of the time their role was
not well-defined. But they were very important for the corporate
image. If not exactly ambulances they were painted white and
decorated with the smart FAU logo. And how could the Unit go
anywhere and do anything if it was not possible to pile into a
truck and set out singing lustily?

Chris Pitt spent almost his entire time at Lavender Farm repairing, maintaining and rebuilding vehicles. Jack Norton's ideal of a multi-seat station wagon, a common enough vehicle in America, had no equivalent over here, but Chris and others did their best with the rebuilding of EYE and GBT ("the big estate with balloon tyres that wandered", he recalls). The newest vehicle was an ex-demonstration model Dormobile. Then there was the jeep. As John Veit Wilson says: "A macho display for a newly licensed adolescent was to drive the white jeep around Melksham and Trowbridge. It had no ignition key; the distributor arm always had to be removed to immobilise it." Alternatively it could be immobilised by rolling over in country lanes. A late and luxurious addition was an Austin Sheerline (GHR), the sort of vehicle that could be bought relatively cheaply once past its first youth

Melksham, 1956: Jack Norton puts the FAU logo on the Leyland bus.
(PHOTO: JOHN PREVETT)

but with a chassis big enough to allow for conversion. Because of uncertainties about the future of the Unit, it never got that far – but perhaps it was a hearse in disguise.

Considering the age of the vehicles and the youth and inexperience of the drivers, serious accidents were mercifully rare. On the way to Vienna in HGH with David Jeffries and a cargo of clothing and penicillin, John Lawson, delayed through engine trouble, drove through the night, fell asleep on the autobahn near Munich, and turned the lorry over. "Fortunately the bales of clothes took the weight and we climbed out unscathed except for a broken windscreen. American servicemen put flares in the road, and one of them said, looking at the lorries and cars pouring past the accident, 'I hate these Hermans!'." Pat Oakley's experience of the Leyland Tiger bus on the same run has been mentioned in the previous chapter. "Because the wretched bus was governed to 30 mph......towards Munich the autobahn goes over hills and I found that we went up hills at 30 mph passing heavily laden German trucks which then whistled past us on the way down. They were clearly mystified by why this white bus... was driven at the same speed downhill as up, and there was much waving and flashing of lights." Derek Smith brought the bus back to England in May 1957 for an overhaul at Borehamwood: "Rudi came with me with some of his furniture, and I am afraid that in Bavaria we shamelessly outdid the Mercedes owners with their folding tables and chairs by eating our picnic lunch in style from a solid oak dining table and matching armchairs temporarily offloaded for the purpose".

On an earlier occasion, described in the 1953 Report, when a lorry with five members, kit and equipment arrived at Benfleet in Essex, "it was the letters FAU that gave us access to Canvey through a police check point when all visitors and potential helpers were being turned away". Yes, the vehicles were important to the outward appearance of the FAUIS.

Entertainment and company

Melksham was not exactly the back of beyond. Bath and Bristol were not far distant, over at Corsham was the Academy of

Art, whose hall of residence at the inappropriately named Monks Court provided the female component at dances and parties, and there were frequently visitors. Already in 1952 Colin Reed was able to report a "fairly good" weekly film programme and rehearsals of "the Lavender Farm Melodrama Group under Colin Sorensen (who always plays the villain) for an entertainment which we hope will amuse Bath Friends at their social tonight". Reginald Reynolds of the Friends Peace Committee, Alex Bryan and Charles Marsh of the Friends Temperance Union, and Jack Eglon were among the visitors, but so also were "boys from the local RAF camp".

There was also sport. As a cricketer from the land of the broad acres, John Blamires found a place in the local team in the summer of 1953. "Playing for Shaw and Whitley was a great experience in many ways, not least of these was establishing a relationship with the local community. That year Shaw and Whitley XI won the cup which was presented by the Melksham Gala queen." Roger Baker and Richard Brown played hockey for Bath Hockey Club. The firm of Pitt and Pittard even joined Bath Rugby Club for one season; could that have been the long-ago foundation of the club's success in today's competitions? And not only sport – David Peryer for a time played the clarinet in the Wiltshire Symphony Orchestra.

On the whole there was less discussion of peace and pacifism than one might have expected. David Maxwell noticed "a facade of cynicism. Intelligent and articulate members puzzled me by their willingness to discuss the world in general... with only passing attention to pacifism. Looking back, I guess that being divided from the rest of society by a tribunal left many of us with unresolved feelings that we chose to leave on hold." Politics was not barred as a subject, nor was religion, but on the whole there was not a great deal of disharmony, surprising in a group of often awkward individuals. Richard Brown wrote home: "Politics here are almost entirely left-wing with one or two exceptions, not generally very vocal. Nevertheless we get more than our ration of good arguments." Bob Stokes, it's true, says there was "a lot of deep discussion going on, most of it on moral and theological matters" and remembers "Christopher Browne exclaiming 'God,

I can't stand being at HQ, you're liable to bump into small groups discussing the trinity'", which sounds a very normal reaction. But then "Christopher Browne did not work in socks but wrapped his feet into disgusting-looking 'footcloths'". That last sounds more like authentic Lavender-Farm-speak.

The Office

A shifting staff which usually included a Cashier or Accountant, a Quartermaster and sometimes an Assistant Secretary, occupied the office. "Once a quarter", Richard Brown recalls, "Henry Ecroyd would visit Melksham, bringing his own pillow because IS ones were so awful, to help the Cashier complete the trial balance – and at the end of the year prepare the annual accounts".

John Veit Wilson spent five months in 1955 there: "The office opened off the common room. Low ceiling, cramped, full of old furniture and filing cabinets. Trevor Hatton (Cashier) was there most of the time. Jack seemed to come and go...".

Here the disposition lists were typed each month, Occasional Information newsletters were prepared, and the system of allowances was administered. Malcolm Page was sent to the Gregg School in Swiss Cottage in November 1953 "for training as a shorthand typist to be 'Records Secretary'" and served in that position for a year from February 1954.

Working there as Quartermaster gave no special privileges, it seems. Roger Bland, in 1954, was one of those who didn't immediately claim his personal allowance of two guineas a month, despite an edict from the Cashier that the whole amount must be claimed each month or be forfeited. The following month he found his request for back pay refused, and on protesting was told he must await a policy relaxation on this one occasion; two days later he received a bag with 504 pennies in it.

The clothing and other allowances were accountable, that is one was paid what one had spent, preferably on presentation of a receipt (what in the Civil Service would be called 'actuals'). This naturally involved a lot of paperwork over what today seem laughably small sums. But what it did was underline the somewhat precarious economy of the Unit as a whole.

The Move from Melksham

By the Summer of 1955 Occasional Information was able to carry news of a proposed move. The Unit was by then in the process of acquiring Tunmers, a house at Chalfont St Peter, Bucks. Over the five years that it had been at Lavender Farm, the emphasis had shifted away from the programme of home industries; pig and poultry keeping had been discontinued and their replacement by the new petrol station involved neither the same space or work commitments. At the same time the amount of hospital and forestry work had increased to the extent that it had been found necessary to restrict activities at HQ. Tunmers offered a base nearer to London and to the forestry sections in the south-east, though it had less than a fifth of the living and storage accommodation at Lavender Farm. But changes in national policy on conscription meant that there was also the likelihood of a drop in membership. In the event, the move took much longer than expected. Delay in taking possession and a further assessment of what needed doing pushed the date into 1956. Former members David Peryer, by then at LSE, David Robson and Ray Ferris called in to help with work at Tunmers. Though clearance work started at Melksham, it was not vacated, and for much of the next year Tunmers was a section rather than the new HQ. Peter Leeming remembers it as "a large house, quasi Art and Crafts, built about 1910, with many bathrooms, including one with a central bath. Jack claimed that the bath had been used by Merle Oberon when she was mistress to Alexander Korda. The extensive grounds had been sold off for commuter housing....". This was why he found himself working on putting in a precast concrete fence to separate off the main house.

Meanwhile back at Melksham the workshops had been suddenly called upon to cope with putting into service seven vehicles for various uses in connection with Hungarian relief work. The split office continued into 1957, by which time the decision had been taken to close down the Unit in July 1959, and membership had already fallen to the extent that forestry work had to be discontinued. In June 1957 the Council took the decision to sell Tunmers, rather than spend any more on its refurbishment, and return to Melksham. For a while Tunmers had become effectively the new HQ, its office staff, including Accounts, coping with the arrangements for the movement of members and the shipment of vehicles and supplies while the focus of work was Vienna. Melksham covered the rest of the administrative work and the resource of the workshops. Three of the five trucks sent out to Vienna were taken there by office staff from HQ.

CHAPTER 10

Conditions of service

WHEN THE FAU Post-War Service was established, in May 1946, the wartime FAU was still in existence, and 47 of its members transferred to the new organisation. The conditions of service were similar: members gave their services free, with the exception of three executive officers, and received maintenance and a nominal pocket-money allowance. The new members coming in were younger, unskilled, and many came straight from school. They were expected to join a training camp. Membership was probationary until the camp and a medical examination had provided an assessment of suitability for the relief work likely to be undertaken. There was no recruitment for specific projects; the expectation was that members would undertake whatever job was required of them – at home or overseas. That was the continuation of "Go Anywhere, Do Anything".

The training camp at Northfield Manor in April 1947 was expected to be the last; plans for PWS did not extend beyond the end of 1948 when the Gordon Square headquarters was to be vacated. By June 1948 the outline of a new scheme of service had been drawn up, as recounted in Chapter 4, but of course any such scheme would need new entrants, and they would need training. The further Manor Farm camp, planned for August 1948, was to last two months or until it was possible to move into the projected new headquarters camp, at that time thought likely to be in Yorkshire.

Again there were similarities in the new service scheme, but prospective members were warned at the outset that they should not look at the new International Service in terms of the war-time FAU. They were also told: "If you come to us straight from a closely defined timetable of school or college studies, you will probably find it difficult at first to adjust yourself to the more precarious nature of our work. Our life is full of the unexpected, long-laid plans often have to be scrapped overnight in the light of some fresh event. The lessons of experience do not run to a set syllabus and most of us have to learn a good deal about ourselves, and how to live with each other, before we can help other people. We have to be endlessly adaptable – in thinking as well as action." Sound advice. The history of the Unit over the next ten years showed just how adaptable it too had to be.

Membership of PWS and FAUIS was limited to young men, conscientious objectors on religious or humanitarian grounds to military service, but it was emphasised that it was not primarily an alternative service for all such objectors. What was considered fundamental was that members shared Quaker views on peace and war, that they accepted the corporate discipline of the organisation, and that they were physically fit and could pass a medical examination. They were expected to serve for a minimum of two years. This tied in with Ministry of Labour requirements; where tribunals imposed conditions, the period was generally two years and two months – the extra two months representing any time that a national serviceman might spend in subsequent training with the Territorial Army or equivalent reserve. These requirements, and those of the Unit, remained consistent throughout the life of FAUIS (see Appendix D for a later version of advice to new members).

The Constitution of PWS and IS, inherited from the FAU, shows that much of the democratic organisation of that body survived in its successors (see Appendix E). When one considers the often awkward and opposite characteristics of the intake, right from the start, it seems to have worked surprisingly smoothly. "My Section Leader I greatly liked and respected", writes Peter Portwood, of the 1st Training Camp in 1946, "and there were others with similar qualities. But a small number of their peers seemed to be among the barmiest people at liberty." Occasionally Standing Orders could give problems. Some ten years later a

GPC ruling against beards – no-one with a beard could be accepted into membership and no member could grow a beard during membership – gave rise to local difficulties. "Great controversy over David Hunt growing a beard", writes John Lawson, then working at Southwater, "he was thrown out of the Unit for a while". But most seem to have accepted that this prohibition, aimed presumably at avoiding superficial judgement of the Unit as a whole from the appearance of individuals, was something they could live with.

Tribunals

Nobody can say the tribunals' job was an easy one; they were supposed to decide, on the basis of a written statement and interview, whether an objector's objection was conscientious or not. But, even with this allowance, they were as uneven in their performance as the cases they were considering. Tribunals could, and quite frequently did, impose conditions, acceptable to some but not to others, and sometimes these specified relief work or even mentioned the FAU, although the Unit never accepted members simply because a tribunal had so directed. There were geographical differences too; without doubt some tribunals (Fulham, for instance) did their best to deserve a reputation as "difficult", just as some objectors were always likely to qualify for that description. There was a right of appeal to a special Appellate Tribunal.

Appearance before a tribunal could take place after a member had joined the Unit. A typical short report from Occasional Information in Spring 1951 reads: "At recent tribunal hearings Keith Wall gained FAU as a conditional registration from the Manchester local; Christopher Browne and John Tempest were similarly registered at London Appellate, but Paul Goldshaft's appeal was dismissed. Terry Ashforth, Hugh Hebert and Ted Millborrow, who were conditionally registered, have been told by the Ministry of Labour that their service with FAU will be regarded as complying with their conditions though it was not specifically recorded."

Quakers would usually have an easier passage than, say, a Seventh Day Adventist, objectors on religious grounds stood a better chance than those raising economic or political arguments, and those prepared to accept some alternative service were usually in a stronger position than those seeking unconditional exemption. But, other than that, it was an unpredictable business. John Veit Wilson, prepared to accept alternative service with FAUIS, was unexpectedly given unconditional exemption, so that instead of joining as a full member for two years, he joined as an associate member for 15 months and was able to go on to university a year earlier than expected. Others found their university plans tacked onto the end of their conditions.

In a letter home, Richard Brown gave an account of his appearance before the Bristol tribunal (local to Melksham) in October 1951: "There were five of us: Roger Baker, Ken Adams, Geoffrey Mitchell, Brian Geeson and myself. I think we were all very nervous and this was worsened by having to wait about an hour on Chippenham station... The Municipal Charities Building is a Georgian building in a Georgian street, and the tribunal was held in a biggish room with dark mahogany tables and chairs... The tribunal entered fairly promptly while we stood up. It consisted of six people: Judge Wethered, a woman member, a trades union delegate, a man who fought on the Somme, a man who was keen on the Old Testament, and one other. The first case was a person called Rutter, a Friend who had just qualified as an accountant and was helping in his father's solicitors business... The firm of Rutter and Rutter was well known to the judge – 'quite straightforward' – and he was exempted conditional upon continuing present work, income tax side of his father's office. The Min. of Labour man quite rightly objected that this was not national service, but the tribunal seemed to think it was.... The next two cases were quite easy; both were prepared to accept non-combatant (duties) and despite some questioning were granted such exemption without hesitation. With the next case the tribunal reserved its decision. Although the fellow did not seem to have thought out his position very carefully, and his witness didn't help, I thought the tribunal, and the judge in particular, once they had the notion that he was physically afraid, were very unfair, hardly giving him a chance to state his case and maintaining, as they did to some of us, that we had no answer to unprovoked aggression. The judge would also not hear of 'thou shalt not kill' but insisted that it was 'not commit murder' and would not allow anyone to use the word 'murder' except in its legal definition....

Roger Baker was next and the first of us five who followed in a string. He was congratulated on his statement, asked questions only about FAU and his future plans. On hearing that he wanted to go to Oxford in '53 this was tacked onto a string of conditions...Altogether we began to feel hopeful. I was next and was 'just the same', 'quite straightforward'. Besides describing one sentence in my statement as ridiculous the judge seemed satisfied....asked me my age and about going to Cambridge. Tom's (Thomas Green – headmaster of Bootham School) letter was read out and helped overweight the balance in my favour... I then gathered I was conditionally exempted and retired to get my 1/6d subsistence allowance and listen to the others... My condition reads as follows: 'As a member of the Friends Ambulance Unit International Service or whole time work on the land in agriculture, horticulture or forestry, or whole time hospital work or after 1 October 1953 as a university student'.... The other three got through almost as easily but I learnt that one shouldn't make one's statement too complicated and if a statement or applicant does not impress favourably letters can be very useful." Particularly if they underlined a Quaker upbringing. Thomas Green is reported to have remarked that one only had to mention Ackworth, Bootham and Quakers and you would be all right!

Roger Bush (Saffron Walden and Bootham) writes: "Although I could not claim to be a convinced Quaker, the tribunal clearly took the view that ten years at Quaker schools had rendered me unfit for anything other than the alternative service option I was seeking. I can't recall any awkward questions...".

Mark Chamberlain, however, remembers his Quaker tag with some embarrassment. At Fulham, after his statement had been read out, there was a short pause and he was asked if he was a "friend" of the previous applicant. When he said he was, without further ado he was given the conditions he needed for service with PWS. As he says: "Almost anywhere else in the world at that time (1947) I would have been imprisoned, or worse".

For some, though, the tribunal was a much more traumatic event. Richard Morley writes: "I had approached the tribunal with the strongest feeling that, if ever I was standing up for God and Jesus, now was the moment and that I would be given the strength to stand up to the 'ordeal'. That I 'got through' was largely thanks to my witness who spoke for me. Shaken and tongue-tied I was awe-inspired, and the stupid questions, about which we had laughed when tribunals were discussed at Brook (hospital section), left me speechless. I felt no hint of a divine presence guiding me. More articulate friends than I were dismissed, and this was no comfort, nor was the theory that 'Christ had spoken for me through the agency of my witness'. (Incidentally my witness – Rev Chick – had previously assisted my father to unconditional exemption many years ago)."

Things did not always proceed smoothly. In the summer of 1950 John Fairfax was writing of his prison experiences: "As a member of FAUIS, in which service I had spent a year doing work I am sure is for national good, I did not imagine the Authorities would transfer me to one of their prisons. But they did, on March 15th, for three months, with a third remission for 'exemplary conduct'. From the Court I was taken to Winchester and there, with the help of some arrogant warders who did their best to humiliate me, ushered into the routine... After I had acclimatised myself to Winchester, I learnt I was to be sent to Lewes for the rest of my sentence – seven weeks. It was during this trip, broken only by a couple of days stay at Wormwood Scrubs (an apt name, as the cell floors are wooden and one spends most of confinement hours scrubbing it), that I realised fully what my companions in crime were like. During the journey I was manacled to a young burglar who, I was told, was 'pretty fair'...He did not tell me the secrets of his trade, just the profits he gained and lost on gambling....". Robin Mills, after twice refusing to submit to medical examination, was also sentenced to three months at Winchester: "We are allowed only three library books a week which doesn't go very far with me so I am spending most of my time reading straight through the Bible. I have got as far as the Book of Ruth...".

In the same year, Derrick Smith, as noted earlier, was also having trouble for refusing a medical examination. Summoned down from Kershopefoot to appear before magistrates at Portsmouth, he "was given an excellent hearing" on 11 October but was nevertheless fined. The following Spring he was prosecuted a second time for the same 'offence', again at Portsmouth, where magistrates cunningly didn't sentence him to a term of imprisonment, but ordered him to visit St James's Hospital, Portsmouth, for a medical examination to determine his fitness for a prison sentence. The case was heard again on 15 May to consider the medical report. This had stated that, in the opinion of the examining doctor, in fact the Royal Navy's MO, he would not be acceptable for military service but that he was suited to continue his work with FAUIS. The MO had discreetly telephoned Jack Norton to confirm that Derrick would be permitted to continue his FAU service. The magistrates then dismissed the case. The prosecuting solicitor indicated that the Ministry of Labour would not again charge Derrick for refusal to undergo a medical examination to comply with the National Service Acts.

Roderick Ogley, as a political activist (he organised a public meeting in Melksham with the title "Korea – Must it go on?" in July 1952), was always going to have a hard passage, as he admits: "I had difficulties with tribunals, chiefly because my objections were neither based on a religion nor applicable to all wars..... As a result of failing to get the conditional exemption I sought, I spent half my FAUIS service waiting for tribunals, actual conscription, and then prison". Registered at Glasgow local tribunal in November 1951 for non-combatant duties in the armed forces, he appealed, lost his appeal in March 1952, was ordered to take a medical examination, refused, and was sentenced in July to six months imprisonment. With a third of the sentence remitted for "good conduct", he was released in November and returned to the Unit, going on from there to work as an organiser for OCFR.

Health, food, leisure, and working conditions

The Unit undertook responsibility for all medical attention, although, like the wartime FAU, it made clear the fact that no compensation could be expected in the event of death or injury while serving. Considering the variety of tasks and some of the living conditions on overseas assignments, the health record was not a bad one. Colin Reed's experience at Plön in 1950 (see Chapter 6) was probably the most serious accident, and jaundice was a problem more than once in overseas sections. It was at Plön too that Julian Gyngell went down with jaundice. "The doctor said I wouldn't catch it", says Simon Cohen, "so I nursed him until I too went down with it. We were then both looked after, very kindly, by Major Preece's wife, 'Die Majorin', until we were well enough to be sent back to Melksham."

The year 1954 produced the worst casualty rate overall. At Southwater several members suffered cuts which turned septic, and at Bromsgrove hay fever was a problem, while in Greece six out of the eleven working there got infections of jaundice and one also contracted amoebic dysentery. Martin Scott had to be repatriated after contracting poliomyelitis; fortunately it was spotted early by a Greek Red Cross sister, he was taken to Athens, and flown home to the Wingfield Hospital, Oxford. Illness that year also hit the training camp programme; mumps at Southwater put the section into quarantine just before the annual camp was due to start at Melksham. As a result, training was staggered, with five smaller groups accepted between August and November.

A course of injections, usually undergone just after the training programme, protected against known risks like tetanus and typhoid, and included BCG jabs as cover against tuberculosis. The dates of these were entered in members' record books along with date and place of Mantoux tests and X-ray examinations. At one time injections were provided by the Medical Officer at the local RAF station.

Spartan living conditions were all very well, but food was fuel for young men engaging in hard, physical work, often in the open air. Not surprising then that it is central to members' recollections, particularly of foreign sections, from the "endless boiled cod and sprouting potatoes" endured in Finnmark to the "soup with big globules of fat" that was part of Hungarian hospitality in Austria more than a decade later.

In post-war France, food was often very poor and dysentery common. Ian Robins's diary at Osny lists both. "Sept.1947 –

(breakfast) only coffee, bread and sugar; Oct., Andrew Rogers and Adrian Parsons go to Belgium for food and return only with chocolate". Later on things improved: "20 May 1948 – 11 ducks and 1 rabbit killed on farm, 21 May – Duck and rabbit for dinner".

Even on home sections the diet could be a bit sparse, particularly in the early days. You had to watch the ration coupons, and food supplies had to be husbanded carefully. FAU catering was handled through the Ministry of Food; the daily routine of forms, coupons, points allocated and returns submitted, was a part of the Unit's civilian status. The largest item on a list of food transferred from Gordon Square to Petersfield in October 1948 is 14lb of custard powder, but with it travelled "one small spam and one small pilchards". A letter of the same date, signed by Mark Chamberlain, the Quartermaster, and addressed to John Rowntree and Sons Ltd of Scarborough, says "We would be pleased to take two dozen 1lb tins of your recommended whale steaks". He recalls that these were inedible and that "the kitchen crew ate alone for several days".

"Food was the most important part of life at this time", writes David Hall, remembering Petersfield in 1949. "Manual work required lots of calories. Thick bread sandwiches, filled mainly with vegetables, and sometimes with cheese, were eaten during the day. Food rationing was still in force, so protein was restricted and often provided by beans, and lentil roasts. Large quantities of potatoes were consumed, and stodgy puddings eaten with gusto... Vast quantities of bread, peanut butter and Marmite accompanied the evening cocoa."

Colin Henderson, at Vercheny, certainly noticed the connection with health: "We lived in a poor community; the food was simple, cheap and of a very limited variety. Those who had been there several months found that the restricted diet meant that the nicks and knocks which come with manual labour just did not heal...". At Plön, Simon Cohen remembers: "We saw groups of children arrive from DP camps and get 'fattened up' at the Kinderheim before being sent back, hopefully stronger to resist disease. I guess we had the same food as they did, which was very basic, except for Sunday breakfast, which was cocoa and cake!

On Saturdays we spent all our pocket money at once, in the town, on coffee and rich cakes."

And when the diet was adequate it could take some getting used to. Bob Stokes in Greece: "Olive oil is the keynote here...cauliflowers were in plentiful supply and oranges and lemons are still available in quantity. A sort of spinach is eaten cooked and soaked in olive oil – an acquired taste! Potatoes are a staple food, often served with oil...". The fruit, at least, would have been welcome in Germany, where a refugee's diet was of low nutritional value. Malcolm Page lists a day's menu at Altenau: "Breakfast – 2 rolls with jam and a slice of bread with dripping; morning snack – 2 slices of bread and a very little broth; lunch – soup, made of potato and turnip; tea – two iced buns and coffee; supper – four slices of bread and coffee". And David Whitworth, in Hanover, wrote home of "waiting in this cafe until the fourth member of the FAU joins us and we are going for a meal; we are to spend some money on meat! What a prospect!". If this makes these overseas members sound like refugees, that is, in effect, what they were. The real refugees had honed their own survival skills; they generally managed to keep warmer and better fed. In Hanover they had their own supply lines in the city and were even able to get fresh fruit if you made it worth their while. Meat was such a rarity that Roger Bush adapted the lines of a student song they were taught: "Horch, was kommt von draussen 'rein? Hollahi, hollaho! 's wird wohl dann der Fleischer sein, hollahi-aho! Geht vorbei und schaut nicht 'rein, wird's wohl nicht gewe-sen sein, hollahiaho!"* but comments: "On this occasion HQ came up trumps and we were given a small allowance to supple-ment the rations".

Songs were part of the work-camp ethic. The International Work Camp Song Book had raided the heritage of folk-songs, student songs, in several languages, and was by no means con-fined to the Mennonite work camps. Malcolm Page's diary records that "we sang jolly work camp songs together in a very cold room". That was in Germany, but Jasper Kay remembers

---

* "Hark, who's that out there? ... It'll be the butcher, then.... Goes right past and doesn't look in.... it won't have been him then!"

that at Champcevrais "In the evenings we sang a lot – a mixed variety of songs from different countries. I painstakingly wrote out the words of these and still have the collection of 50-60 songs." Malin Bergman, who was sent by her parents, Swedish Quakers, to join the Champcevrais community during the summer holidays in 1952, and later married FAUIS member Bernard Andrews, who was also there in 1952, has written: "And then we sang! Song after song, and if there were people from other countries, they might be asked to sing one in their own language. So there were quite a few English songs I learned too." Anyone who could play a guitar was especially welcome. And yet, as far as can be discovered, the FAU esprit de corps produced no songbook and not even a song.

Any plans for leisure necessarily had to be of a short-term nature. Although some of those members whose particular skills made them valuable for longer periods of service at HQ were able to join clubs and take part in local activities (see chapter 9), as a rule the uncertainty caused by the need for short-notice transfers frustrated any continuing commitments. The GADA principle, in part supported by these uncertainties, was less of a worry to members than it might appear. Living from day to day when you are in your late teens or early twenties is a strain accepted by most, whether students or national servicemen. Included in the joining instructions was a reminder that members should be able to carry their own clothing and equipment for a distance of a mile on foot. Working clothing and footwear weighed around 20 lbs, so there was no great incentive to overcrowd a rucksack or suitcase with personal possessions.

Boiler suits and battledress were still popular items of clothing in PWS days, generally a dark blue, though a white version was available for the kitchen. PWS uniform provided two sets of clothing – "a No.1 outfit for smart jobs and for 'walking out' when off duty, and a No.2 outfit for manual work" – and hints were given to new entrants on how to wear the No.1 outfit correctly. Any old Army or Civil Defence buttons were to be removed and black ones sewn on instead, together with flashes, appropriately spaced. Berets were then part of standard uniform. "Always wear your beret..... Put it on at first dead straight about an inch and a half above the eyebrows and with the bow at the back. Then pull down on the right hand side. Your PWS badge should be pinned to the front." And finally: "Carry a small clothes brush in your kit – the dark blue battledress shows the dirt very easily".

Gum boots and greatcoats were general issue for outdoor work, the emphasis being always on strong, inexpensive clothing; government surplus items were obtainable without sacrificing clothing ration coupons. Khaki battledress tunics and trousers could be dyed, though the colour options were limited – navy blue and deep burgundy were the most successful. Ex-army clothing continued to be useful well into the years of IS. It could be bought in bulk quantities at WD sales.

Working conditions were a known quantity in hospital or forestry sections, with only minor local variations. On overseas sections things were more complicated; other agencies had different standards, and a workforce made up of several different nationalities, while it might help build international understanding, was not always the best choice for building anything else. As early as 1947 an interchange scheme in Carinthia, where members were to work alongside Austrian students in supplying labour on farms, ran into problems when the students were dissatisfied with the working conditions arranged locally and decided to leave. With the interchange basis lost, the PWS team had to retire to Vienna to help an international group engaged in clearing the war-damaged buildings of a children's hospital.

Though the income from the farm work carried out around Petersfield was important in the early years of IS, that was not the only reason for engaging in this kind of work, as has already been noted in Chapter 4. For there was then a belief that understanding the life of the agricultural worker was much more important to promoting understanding between nations than would be the case today, when agriculture almost everywhere employs fewer and fewer people. (Perhaps this was a more far-sighted view than it seems, given the divisive effects on international relations of the Common Agricultural Policy!) And while some of the outworkers progressed to driving tractors and milking as well as general farm work, it was largely unskilled labour.

While some training could be given in specialised building construction, such as that involved in post-earthquake work in Greece, usually building skills were acquired on the job and from foremen and skilled workers in charge of projects.

Finally all members on joining became aware that the running of the organisation involved its members in acting as cooks, orderlies, clerks, secretaries – by and large they were their own support staff.

CHAPTER 11

Members' impressions of FAU PWS/IS

A CIRCULAR LETTER to all those recorded as having served in FAU Post-War Service and International Service invited them to set down how they saw the Unit, how it met their needs at the time, and how it affected their lives subsequently. This chapter is based mainly on the response to that invitation.

In responding, several members acknowledged the debt they owed to the Unit, its members and all those who created and ran PWS and IS in best Quaker tradition.

For most of those faced with national service and looking to the FAU as an alternative to the armed forces for whatever reasons, there was a genuine desire for the variety of opportunity that it offered in comparison with employment in agriculture or in hospitals which might be made a condition of registration as a conscientious objector. There were some grumbles that International Service was not as international as its name implied, but service overseas was never promised as of right. All the same, within the limitations of enough work being available in foreign sections, most members were able to do some of their work there.

Sometimes expectations did not run too high. Roderick Ogley writes: "When I applied to join FAUIS for two years, I hoped to find a socially useful alternative to the military service the state was demanding of me, but I did not expect to enjoy the experience. Looking at it from society's point of view, it seemed reasonable that, if exempted from the soldiering that was imposed on practically every other man of my age, I should be required to perform a stint of similar length, and similarly tedious, low-ranking and ill-paid.... I felt that during my service in FAUIS, assuming I got the conditional exemption I sought, I would be contributing indirectly, and perhaps at times also directly, to socially worthwhile projects, but that in the process I would be bored stiff."

As recorded earlier, Roderick did not get the conditional exemption he sought, but by the time he had exhausted the appeal procedure and was facing prison, his opinions about the Unit had changed: "there was a period, once I had come to terms with the failure of my appeal and the inevitability of prison, when I could not plan more than about a week ahead, and thus really did have to live in the present, when each new day in the company of, or in contact with, my friends inside and outside FAUIS had an extraordinary preciousness to it, which I have never experienced since".

For Jesse Hillman, his brief service with PWS (1946) was an ideal way to end his time with the FAU. "I was able to share something of what I had learned, I felt that I was in at the outset of a body which would carry on the spirit of the Unit which had been my life for several years, and I enjoyed the continuing close comradeship of the FAU before I moved on to begin my missionary training."

Brian Wills (1946-48) pays special thanks to "all those who created and ran PWS and the International Service that followed". A member of the first PWS training camp he recalls: "For an 18-year-old, fresh from Quaker school, joining the PWS naturally represented a stimulating way of making contact with the outside world in a pacifist (and therefore somewhat protected) context. I retain an immense sense of gratitude that there existed such people as Jack Eglon and Ian Robinson who took it upon themselves to maintain the FAU tradition in its new PWS form, and through their drive and organisational abilities made it possible for young National Service entrants like myself to opt for two years working with PWS in European countries." Of his service, he adds: "For good measure, it started a love-affair with

France sustained over the years that has ended in permanent residence in the country".

Giles Heron (1946-48) also served in France, and writes of his time at Les Mesnuls: "What we gained individually in social and cultural experience outweighed whatever service we rendered, but I like to think that through the balance of the two we contributed something worthy of the FAU PWS purpose of improving international understanding in those difficult years".

Another early PWS member, who had joined the FAU in its closing months, and was also at Les Mesnuls, was Brian Priestman (1946-48). For him it was "more of the family tradition (after all, my father's favourite brother was killed in the FAU in 1918...)". But he adds: "Looking back I feel sure that had I known more about what was really happening in Germany, what was politically, socially and morally going to happen in Britain and the rest of Europe had everyone laid down their arms in the interests of Pacifism, then I suspect my views, and many other people's views too, would have been different at the moment of conscription. We were all so young, so naive, so ignorant of any life beyond the cocoon of school and family and Meeting. So my immediate needs were met. My passions and convictions about the sort of life I was going to lead, were interrupted for three years, and I was conscious of that. That my time in the FAU affected my life after leaving it I do not believe for one moment, other than that it gave me the opportunity to learn about the ways of life as seen by continental Europeans, to become an internationalist, that it gave me too an opportunity to speak colloquial French, which has remained a part of my life, and that I learned how to drive a car, and to gain some experience in compassion, caring and the real needs of others." (That is some catalogue, though.)

Fred Deutsch (1946-48) writes: "I would like to pay tribute to Gordon Square's efforts to cope with a very square peg. Almost all PWS was straight out of Friends' boarding schools, and the ethos reflected this. I had only been in the UK seven years, living with a parson's family, whose ministry was exclusively in slums... I had had no previous contact with such a bourgeois environment.... Also I had been working for the preceding five years, and whilst I could not claim more maturity, I think in some ways I was more street-wise. Putting McCann (John D McCann) and me together was an excellent stroke; he too was from a non-Friends, not very middle-class, background, had practical experience of employment, and we happen to share an interest in the visual arts.... I am grateful to PWS for introducing me to the work-camp movement in which I remained active for some years after 1949."

Horst-Eckehart Höhne (1947-48) was among the German associate members who joined the PWS: "it definitely broadened my thinking and my views in an early and decisive phase of my life", he writes, adding "it was a basic experience in years in which it was extremely difficult to get this experience without help".

"Membership of PWS meant a great deal to me" writes Denis Earp (1947-49). "Thanks to my five years at Bootham, I was well equipped to make the most of the opportunities which PWS gave me to become a more mature person whilst providing what I believed to be a worth-while service to others. PWS gave me leadership opportunities I had not had at school, as well as the chance to work in France for nearly a year. IS enabled me to make lasting friendships with one or two Germans in England. I found my final months at Petersfield something of an anti-climax after the more varied time with PWS. I owe much to Jack Eglon's leadership and friendship through my period of service."

For many, perhaps too many, the Unit formed a natural progression from a Quaker upbringing, and more specifically from Quaker schools. David Gray (1950-52) writes: "An immensely valuable two years, as well as exciting and enjoyable. A wonderful 'sandwich filling' between leaving school (Bootham), aged almost 19, and going to college (Merton, Oxford) on my 21st birthday....Britain's universities generally must have benefited from receiving new students who had mostly had two years' experience of national service.." However, he adds "My Bootham contemporaries who did their two years with the Forces often found it stimulating, but many spoke also of two years' boredom, or useless activities, and said the army had taught them how to dodge work and responsibility, and had schooled them in only social survival techniques. My own two years was blessedly different: thanks to the COs of an earlier generation, to the founders of FAU, to an enlightened tribunal, to the Society of Friends. What an inheritance. For me FAUIS was not so much a time of Quaker witness...or of building international peace... Much more it was an educational adventure...".

For Colin Henderson (1950-52) "It was in the Quaker inspired atmosphere at Bootham that I became clear that, when National Service was due, I would be a CO. After leaving school therefore, I was only at work five months before joining FAUIS in February 1950... FAUIS was my tertiary education. There I met and had to work with all sorts of people I had not encountered before, both those from wealthy and privileged backgrounds and those from impecunious and artisan backgrounds. I also had to undertake tasks and assume responsibilities that were totally new to me.... All in all, the FAU experience broadened my horizons and made me more self-reliant. I am not sure that at 18/19 I was aware of 'the underlying philosophy of members'. I probably gained more from it than I contributed to it."

David Hall (1949-51) was also with the IS in its early years: "The Unit was the making of me as an independent person. I came from a sheltered background and had never been away from home. In the Unit I developed views of my own, and self-reliance. I also learnt self-discipline and the fact that hard manual work never did anyone any harm! I learnt that it is possible to put ideals into action. As a result of my experiences – particularly at Le Court – I decided to change course and go into medicine. You will see that the Unit had a profound effect in my life and this is a tribute to the philosophy and ideals."

The same is true of Ray Ferris (1950-52), who writes: "There is no doubt that the Unit had a profound effect on shaping my future. After leaving the service in May 1952, I worked at this and that for a couple of years, including six months as a machine shop inspector, but I could no longer stand being cooped up in a factory, having spent all my youth in one. I studied social science at LSE for two years on a diploma course....". After visiting relatives in the USA, Ray took up social work in British Columbia, specialising in child protection.

Richard Brown (1951-53), who listed a number of ways in which his FAUIS experience had affected his life, included "doing manual work on a daily basis for the only occasion in my life (so far!)", paid a couple of personal tributes "Thanks to Bryan Reed, a qualified accountant, I acquired an excellent training in book-keeping and some understanding of accounts" and "thanks largely to David Peryer I learnt to drive and passed my test", and added that "the Unit's ideals – of international service, of being prepared to tackle unfamiliar tasks, of working co-operatively in non-hierarchical structures, and so on – have remained important to me; and friendships made in IS have been some of the most important in my life". He also points out that "being a conscientious objector would have been much more uncomfortable if it (FAU PWS/IS), or a close equivalent, had not existed – and that would be the case several times over in wartime".

Jasper Kay (1952-54) says "The FAU gave me a life-long interest in work camps (where I met my wife!) and a real enjoyment of making do with a simple life", and also discovers "one negative influence, because I went on to study at Cambridge and hated it! The values subconsciously absorbed during the previous two years were suddenly negated by the artificiality and the prodigal nature of University life".

"Looking back," says David Barkla (1952-54) "I feel my own 'philosophy' at the time was lamentably naive and narrow. The Unit gave me a great deal of food for thought, much of which I didn't digest until later, if at all. But I think it's fair to say FAUIS had almost no means of propagating its principal values, or even its most valued traditions. That was a pity; the Unit was in some ways a new social institution, but socially retarded people like me got only sporadic glimpses of that, not an empowering vision."

"Whilst the decision to register as a CO was", writes Colin Gilbraith (1953-55), "fundamental to all my life subsequently, I cannot be sure I would have taken it so easily had the FAUIS not been in existence; and the 'life skills' experience in the Unit, the sense of belonging and enjoyment in doing serious work in a

cheerful manner, and many friends, have been enduring conse-
quences of membership". He goes on to point out that "the work
of the Unit played a significant role in gaining from non-pacifists
some understanding of the motivation of pacifists and their convictions, and was therefore important in a very wide context".

With a year at University between leaving school and joining
the Unit, Roger Bush (1953-55) was "somewhat disconcerted to
find so many ex-Bootham and other Friends' school leavers
among the company; it was like reverting to boarding school all
over again". He writes: "I think I learned a great deal in a fairly
painless way over my FAUIS service. How to pace yourself in
labouring jobs, the disciplines of hospital work, the sort of gulf
between perception and reality where refugees were concerned, a
grasp of a greater Europe beyond these shores, a realisation that
idealists and practical types both have their place in the scheme of
things: these are what it can take a lifetime to discover in normal
circumstances. No, the FAUIS was not a normal circum-
stance...".

John Veit Wilson (1954-55) however, rightly emphasises that
"this activity was 'normality' for some others of us, even if it was
numerically unusual by comparison with the millions who passed
through the armed forces". "I had been at a Quaker school
(Saffron Walden) for twelve years from six to eighteen" he writes
"and FAU was very much the expected next step, which several
friends were also taking. I had already attended several Quaker
work camps and both the lifestyle and type of work of FAU thus
presented no great challenge. It seemed then, and still seems, the
right thing to do...".

For Geoffrey Braithwaite (1954-56) "The FAU met my
needs admirably and made a very important contribution to my
personal development. If I had taken deferment (which I was
entitled to do, but chose not to) I would, as it turned out, have
escaped National Service altogether, but I regard it as two years
extremely well invested."

The returns from that investment were not financial, as John
Hume (1954-56) has noted: "At the time, as idealistic, and naive,
18-19-year-olds, money wasn't particularly important to us....

the 10s.6d. a week was sufficient unto the day. I do remember searching out the smallest and cheapest cigarettes (tiny filter tips with names like de Rezke, and Wills Woodbines in paper packs of 5). We knew that the hospital sections, where we earned £8 a week, and the forestry sections (income less certain but could be high if we had an especially competent team on piece-rate) provided the financial basis for Unit activities elsewhere..... that we would have three to six months of international relief work during our two years."

Writing from Pleasant View Bruderhof, Ulster Park, NY, Martin Johnson (1954-56): "It was a wonderful time of hard work in forestry and hospital, and first longer experience abroad (in Greece) – experiences I have never forgotten and value and treasure to this day. It was also through the Unit that I met up with the Bruderhof which later became my life commitment to a way of life consistent with the early Christians of the Acts of the Apostles and early Quakerism – a gift of inestimable value."

And from British Columbia, Fred Cooke (1955-57): "I have kept my pacifism to this date, though not my formal Quakerism. Increasingly I have been applying my work in evolutionary biology to an understanding of the human condition and theism can have no place in my approach, so I suppose I could be described as a Quatheist, since my Quaker experience taught me a lot about how to work and interact with others."

"A positive and formative experience" is how Richard Jones (1955-57) describes his two years with FAUIS. "Two important factors influenced my decision to apply to join the Service, besides the requirements of the National Service Acts and the ruling out of the absolutist position. The first was a family background deeply rooted in the Nonconformist religious tradition; the second, my older brother's registering his objection to military service on grounds of conscience in 1949. Both of us heard about the Unit during the Second World War. One member of the chapel congregation in North Wales to which we belonged as a family, served with the FAU China Convoy. During the war one was aware of the dislocation in the lives of many of our contemporaries. We studied with evacuees from the large industrial cities of Northern England, and with refugees whose strange-sounding surnames indicated that their families had probably fled from continental Europe. But the scale and utter destructiveness of war was not brought home to me directly and vividly for another decade. That happened on a train journey via Cologne to a student conference in Heidelberg in 1954 – a year before joining the FAUIS."

Chance played more of a hand for Owen Cole (1955-57): "I cannot be sure how I came to hear of the FAU. Not from my father who was a Congregational minister and sympathetic to the Quakers and pacifism. Perhaps from Jack Dobbs, a Quaker who was organist at the church which I attended in Durham where I was at University. I had long held pacifist beliefs but had not decided how to put them into effect when it became my turn to face conscription. I had some intention to become a Bevin boy, but national service down the pit was an alternative which was withdrawn just before I graduated. The merchant navy was another possibility, but corporate living with other pacifists had an attraction which led to me contacting Jack Norton and having an interview in London.... At the same time as I was serving with the FAU one of my brothers was doing his national service in the RAF. There is no doubt whose path was of greater worth."

"The FAUIS experience was very important for me" writes Chris Lawson (1955-57) "both for the sense of involvement in worthwhile work at the time, especially the work at Linz, and for the lasting awareness of the situations encountered. I gained useful practical skills, not least from the time being cook at HQ, and a smattering of German. I felt that we were the Unit, left to get on with our lives in each section, with Jack Norton an essential background figure. I know that I felt I had much more experience when I arrived at University...I was glad I had taken the chance for national service when I was 18 and not deferred."

There's another tribute to Jack Norton from John Daw (1956-58), who writes: "I doubt whether a day has passed since 1958 without pleasant memories of my spells at Malvern, Hackney and Linz passing through my mind. For some reason their vividness does not seem to fade – my collection of photos from the Linz section is a prized possession, but seldom looked at since it hardly needs to be.... No doubt I was very fortunate in the people I was with and the work I was doing; certainly I was more than ready, in 1956, for a period of release from the selfish burden of carving out a 'future'. However I am also aware (though we seldom met) of how much I owe to Jack Norton for running the kind of organisation in which I have felt more at home than in any other before or since, and ensuring that, at a time when I was still capable of promising 'to go anywhere and do anything', I was so well rewarded for it."

"Although I had attended Harrow Quaker meeting a few times" writes Alan Quilley (1956-58), "I had never come to know any Quakers before joining the Unit and so this must have had a significant effect on my life as I eventually joined the Society, having rejected my Methodist upbringing". He found it "extremely valuable to have those two years in which to mature and have some of the corners knocked off before going to university", but adds: "At the time I was very disappointed (and still am) not to have been taught some useful practical skills like motor maintenance or building – even elementary first aid. I seemed to have missed a lot by not attending a training camp. Obviously I picked up a few skills as I went along, but I suppose the romantic GADA philosophy had led me to believe that we would get a real training in a particular skill area (as you would in the army)."

For Richard Morley (1956-58) too, his encounter with FAUIS transformed his views about Quakers. "Up to that time I had (perhaps understandably) viewed them as a load of boring old fuddy-duddies who one met from time to time at the quiet rural meeting houses that I attended with my parents as a child. The FAU showed them in a totally different light – a dynamic, highly idealistic, group of young men, the effectiveness of their social witness being completely out of proportion to their numbers. Young men who truly followed the advice to 'live adventurously'" (but they weren't all Quakers – Ed.). "To some extent I was able to continue this vitality into the life of Cardiff meeting...".

"The experience of working in hospitals" says David Elliott (1957-59), another writing from British Columbia, "has meant that I prefer not to go anywhere close to them..". Not so forests, for although David joined too late to work at the last of the forestry sections, he travelled to Denmark and Sweden looking at forestry just after leaving the Unit, and went on to UCNW where he graduated in the subject. He also returned, for two successive summers to Linz to assist with the continuation of work done by FAUIS there. After emigrating to Canada in 1966 he has worked mostly as a forester with the Ministry of Forests in the government of BC.

Euan Pearson (1956-58) was another who returned to a continental section after leaving the Unit (see Chapter 6). "The Unit" he writes "gave me lasting friendships (I was Nick Evens's Best Man, he was mine) and a perspective on life that has been a rock ever since. I'm no longer a Friend and I couldn't hold the strict pacifist line. If I caught someone raping my sister, I'd have no compunction about putting a bullet through his head – except I haven't got a gun. Come to think of it, I haven't got a sister either."

He goes on to add: "I believe national service is no bad thing, provided it's neither military nor conscripted. Both my children have chosen to work abroad, inspired – or so I like to think – by my example. And recently, at the ripe age of 58, I've just done it all again – with VSO in Ghana – with my wife (who also did VSO at 18 and would have made an excellent FAU). We found the same dedication, idealism and youthful enthusiasm among today's 20-30-year-olds (and 40-60-year-olds). I even managed to stay the course. So I guess my message to all FAUIS members who haven't got it out of their system is you can still Go Anywhere Do Anything with VSO. And you don't have to be 18, they take you up to 70. How about it?".

CHAPTER 12

What happened next

B Y THE END OF 1956 it was clear that the end of conscription was coming, and in 1957 the decision was taken to
cease FAUIS operations by the end of July 1959. New members
were accepted only on the basis of associate membership until
that date. Though numbers had started to dwindle, there was no
corresponding reduction in the need for the service that FAUIS
could supply – overseas opportunities were still presenting themselves, and refugee work in Europe continued. So it was also clear
that the Unit could remain active and committed until closure.

There were always some who felt that the existence of FAUIS
should not be a product of the National Service legislation, but at
the same time it had to be faced that the repeal of that legislation
would severely affect recruitment. The Chairman of the FAU
Council wrote, in introducing the report for 1958, the last complete year: "The work of the Unit (FAU) and its successors .... is
no mean achievement, but we can all be thankful that with the
end of conscription it can at last be closed down". That was a
view reflecting a belief among Council members that other
organisations, such as IVSP, provided sufficient opportunity for
service and were also capable of taking up any of the work that
FAUIS was engaged in. At its June 1959 meeting, the Council
agreed that its work was concluded; its members and officers
resigned after appointing trustees to oversee any remaining capital. Paul S Cadbury, who had been its Chairman for twenty years,
thanked Jack Norton "for having charge of International Service
activities for the past nine years when, with a much younger

membership, he had had little opportunity to share the responsibilities....".

At that same meeting Jack Norton had given an account of
the run-down of FAUIS activities. Only three members remained
at home sections and ten at Linz in Austria. Their membership
would terminate on or before 31 July and they would either continue in other work that satisfied their national service conditions
or leave to go to university, apart from five who wished to stay at
Linz until the expiry of their national service commitments.

In the last chapter a former member laments the fact that
FAUIS "had almost no means of propagating its principal values,
or even its most valued traditions". This may have seemed so at
the time, but the later dispersal of ex-PWS/IS members to a wide
variety of differing careers must surely be taken into account. All
carried with them the seeds of their own experience in the organisation.

While there is no statistical record of subsequent employment, it's clear that a fair number went into teaching. John Gray
became headmaster of Bootham School, like his father before
him, Colin Henderson its Bursar, and Gerard Wakeman taught
there; David Gray was a lecturer at Woodbrooke; Keith Newson
and Bob Stokes also became headmasters and Malcolm Elliott
retired after thirty years in teaching. Others, in further and higher
education, included Ron Atkinson, Richard Brown, Basil
Mogridge, Fred Cooke, Malcolm Page, John Veit Wilson, David
Birmingham, John Blamires and John Geale; Colin Gilbraith was
Bursar of Pembroke College, Cambridge, and Thomas Braun is
Dean of Merton College, Oxford. Peter Portwood and Nicholas
Evens went into educational psychology.

Other occupations that emerge from correspondence with
members are medicine, the health and social services, forestry
and horticulture, the arts and communications. David Hall went
into medicine and became a general practitioner largely through
the influence of his time at Le Court. Experience in hospitals led
to John Atherton becoming a surgeon (now in Western Samoa),
David Milne entering nursing, and David Robson and Hugh
Norwood training as hospital administrators. Doig Simmonds

became a hospital artist. The social services attracted, among others, Ray Ferris, Richard Errington, Raymond Penrose, and David Peryer, the last becoming Director of Social Services for Humberside. David Elliott, as noted, became a forester, and Timothy Solloway is concerned with organic horticulture. In Germany, Horst-Ekkehart Höhne studied forestry at Göttingen, Freiburg and Hamburg, afterwards joining the state forest administration in Schleswig-Holstein. Mike Abbatt's experience with the Bedford trucks later led him to become an HGV driver. Richard Taylor and Mark Chamberlain, both cooks and quarter-masters in PWS days, went into food and catering (working for most of his career with a specialised food importer, Mark found himself handling thousands of items, including Chocolat Menier from France). Frank Lees went into the chemical industry (and subsequently into University teaching and research), and Philip Brown into the construction industry. Peter Dyson became an engineer specialising in soil science, David Butler, Brian King and Keith Tyler architects. Tony Bristow's involvement with the science of paper and printing took him to the Swedish Pulp and Paper Research Institute in Sweden, where he still lives. David Andrews has worked for over 30 years as an astronomer at Armagh Observatory, NI. Howard Brunton became an expert on fossil brachiopods, working at the Natural History Museum, and Colin Sorensen an art historian and curator of the modern sections at the Museum of London. Alan Bowness, after teaching at the Courtauld Institute, became Director of the Tate Gallery.

Hugh Hebert and the late Christopher Driver (long-time editor of The Good Food Guide) became Guardian journalists, Kaye Whiteman is still a working journalist on West Africa, John Whitney headed Capital Radio and later became Director General of the IBA, Nick Hudson went into publishing and Euan Pearson into film-making. John McCann became a professional photographer and an expert on timber-framed buildings, and Paul Fox, whose photographs of the Austrian refugee camps were used for publicity purposes, also made photography his career. Brian Priestman established an international reputation as an orchestral conductor and now conducts mainly in USA, living in the mid-West. Paul Diamond joined the staff of UN in 1964 and spent thirty years wrestling with its finances; Jonathan Barkas has been with the Council of Europe for almost as long, and is still living in Strasbourg. Foreign affairs became the specialist subject of Horst Diering, who now lives in Switzerland. Roderick Ogley taught international relations at Aberdeen and Sussex for 33 years.

Altogether, the careers of former PWS/IS members – even from this inadequate (1997) survey – make an impressive list for so small an organisation. As to them carrying forward its values, here is David Morrish: "I have been a councillor for many years. There was the occasion when the local community was flooded and it was evident that there would not be an immediate response from the emergency services. I set about arranging a warm centre for the elderly with hot drinks from the Salvation Army while the Royal Marines deployed their portable heaters to dry out the homes. When the emergency services arrived they told me I had done a good job and asked which training programme I had been on. I replied 'GADA with the FAU'. They didn't enquire more but seemed impressed."

Over the thirteen years of PWS and IS, membership never exceeded 100 at any one time. These figures included, particularly in the earlier years, associate members, most coming from Germany. Three hundred and forty names from PWS and IS were listed in the 1960 FAU register of names and addresses. That is a total less than half of the strength of the wartime FAU in 1945 and not much more than a quarter of the numbers who served in the Unit over the war years.

Ronald Joynes acted as Registrar following that first register compiled by Jack Norton, and he was succeeded by Brian Livesey by the time a second register was produced in 1975. Deryck Moore took over the register, together with the organisation of several reunions, and kept it until 1996, when David Peryer replaced him.

A Management Committee continues (1997) to administer the remaining funds of the FAU, which has retained its charitable status. It maintains the Register of Members, and has made grants in furtherance of its original objectives – the largest being made in 1994 at the end of the Gulf War, when the Committee decided to give nearly all its accumulated assets (£45,000) to the Quaker Peace Service of the Society of Friends for use in relief and rehabilitation work in the former war zone.

As was noted in the introductory notes to both registers, "several groups hold regular reunions and maintain their own address lists". Despite the relatively small numbers, IS members established a pattern of annual reunions held at the Penn Club. Their 1954 reunion recommended that all ex-members should pay a minimum subscription of 5s. a year "for the continuing work of the Service, which also ensures receipt of Occasional Information", and there was a fairly good response. PWS came more firmly into the frame later, when first Sandy Parnis and then Deryck Moore (WW2 FAU and PWS) organised a series of larger residential reunions for all FAU ex-membership – one at Birmingham and three at York, the last as recently as 1996.

It has to be said that PWS/IS attendance at these major reunions was at first minimal; the gatherings came to be seen as first and foremost an opportunity for those with war-time service to get together – the China Convoy members, for instance, are still a very cohesive group. But sixty-seven from PWS/IS attended the 1996 York reunion, perhaps a reflection of the fact that many had by then reached retirement age!

Reunions are not necessarily just for remembering the past. At each there has been earnest discussion about the possibility of reviving a voluntary service organisation along the lines of FAU PWS/IS. Rather than looking backward, David Birmingham would like "the Unit to look forward to the millennium and find ways of creating jobs to foster the idealism of the armies of youths who are living in cardboard boxes under Waterloo Station". Despite Euan Pearson's VSO experience (see Chapter 11), Donald Wride laments: "It seems such a pity these days that overseas service only wants young people with pieces of paper, when there are so many good young people with time on their hands and so much to give and so much to learn about life, as I am sure we all did in those two years". And Robert Woolley writes: "I still think there is a good case for a Quaker-based organisation to cater for volunteers full-time between school and

*Former FAU Post-War Service and International Service members
at York Reunion, 1996.*

(PHOTO: ROGER BUSH)

university doing something useful. No lack of projects. Must be
some money lurking in some old Quaker account. No Leader, I
suppose. They are rare!". Jeremy Cusden thinks "two years of
community service at the age of eighteen is an excellent idea" –
presumably as long as it is not acquired through a criminal sentence.

Any future for an organisation that could carry on FAU traditions raises rather more difficult questions. There is certainly less
scope in modern war and post-war zones for the dedicated
amateur. For one thing it has to be accepted that today's armed
forces are more likely to find themselves on 'peace-keeping'
duties than on offensive actions. Indeed it is arguable that their
training in the use of weapons should be supplemented, or even
replaced, by training in diplomacy, negotiation and reconstruction skills. Might the Ministry of Defence become one day the
Ministry of Defence and Reconciliation, with a strong pacifist

wing? It's not too fantastic a thought. Then, perhaps, some percipient historian will turn up the record of a task force, forged in war-time but with a continued life under peace-time conditions, and see what lessons can be learned.

The introduction to this brief history explained how it arose from a wish by former members of FAU PWS and IS that there should be some published record of an exercise in peace-time pacifism, and how most of the content of this book is based on the responses to an appeal for information, photographs, and memorabilia. The intention is that these will form part of an archive to be housed, with existing records of the war-time Units, at Friends House in London. The archive will contain a complete set of annual reports, accounts, and copies of Occasional Information, the Unit's news-sheet, plus minutes of the meetings of the Council and General Purposes Committee, but these will be fleshed out by the contributions from individual members. Not exactly a regimental museum, but at least a quarry for any future research. Which, as Tony Bristow said (see Chapter 8), is where we came in....

Appendices

A: LIST OF MEMBERS OF FAU POST-WAR SERVICE AND FAU INTERNATIONAL SERVICE, 1946-1959

THE FOLLOWING members of the 1939-45 FAU transferred into the FAU Post-War Service or returned to assist
PWS or IS in an executive capacity between 1946 and 1959.

John (Donald) Andrews
Ronald Atkinson
Maurice Bailey
Dudley Barlow
Brian Bone
Susie Carter (see Moorhouse)
Giles Cooper
Brian Cosford
Kenneth Cue
Dorothy Cuninghame
  (née Stapleton)
Donald Davis
Ralph Eames
Lewis Edwards
C Jack Eglon
John Eveleigh
Derek Gaffee
Alan Gilderdale
Michael Gilderdale
Jesse Hillman

John Hudson
Richard Ingle
Alan King
John King
Ernest Kirk
Anthony Law
Michael Lee
Stuart Lomax
David Long
Raymond Mann
Brian Meara
Deryck Moore
Susie Moorhouse (née Carter)
Leslie Morris
John Murphy
Christopher Nickalls
Jack Norton
Leonard Parker
Edward Parry
Brian Priestman

131

Anthony Richmond
Ian C Robinson
David Rutter
Alan Sarfas
Johan Schneider
David Scott
Geoffrey Soar
George Spencer
Dorothy Stapleton
  (see Cuninghame)

Eric Steele
Thomas (Sam) Stevens
John Swindale
Brian Taylor
Gordon Taylor
Edward Whitaker
Rollo Woods

TOTAL 52

The following list of those who served only in PWS and IS has been compiled mainly from the Registers printed in January 1960, less than a year after the end of activities, and July 1975.

Michael Abbatt
Kenneth Adams
Christopher Alexander
Stephen Alexander
David Ambler
Bernard Andrews
David Andrews
David Artiss
Terence Ashforth
John Atherton
Donald Atkinson
Anthony Back
Malcolm Bagnall
Michael Bailey
Roger Baker
Jonathan Barkas
David Barkla
Simon Barley
Nicholas Barrington
John Benson
Denis Binns
David Birmingham
Roderick Blackburn

Eric Blakeley
John Blamires
Roger Bland
Arthur Boorne
Ernest Bowcott
Brian Bowmer
Alan Bowness
Peter Bradley
Geoffrey Braithwaite
Thomas Braun
David Brewer
J Anthony Bristow
Peter Brown
Philip Brown
Richard Brown
Christopher Browne
Denis Browne
Howard Brunton
Colin Buggey
David Burrows
Gerald Burt
Anthony Burtt
Roger Bush

David Butler
Ben Buxton
Thomas Campbell
Paul Castle
Adrian Chadburn
Mark Chamberlain
John Charter
Roy Chatterton
Alan Chisholm
Francis Clark
John Brian Clark
John Horne Clark
Russell Cleaver
Peter Clery
Simon Cohen
William Owen Cole
David Collinson
Nicholas Conway
John Cook
Fred Cooke
Peter Copeland-Watts
Peter Cornwell
Keith Cottam
Peris Coventry
Alan Cox
Timothy Crow
Robert Culling
Jeremy Cusden
Alan Davies
John Daw
Harold Dellar
Fred Deutsch
Paul Diamond
Robert Diamond
Robin Ditchburn
John Donovan
John Drage
Christopher Driver

Scott Dunbar
John Dunnicliff
Leslie Durham
Richard Durling
Bernard Dursley
Peter Dyson
Ted Dyson
Denis Earp
Keith Eckersley
Raymond Efemey
David Elliott
Malcolm Elliott
Michael Ellis
Richard Errington
Crispin Eurich
Nicholas Evens
David Fairbanks
John Fairfax
Philip Fenton
Ray Ferris
Alan Fincham
Peter Firth
Paul Fox
Jonathan Franklin
John Gaskin
John Geale
Brian Geeson
Colin Gilbraith
Rodney Giles
Ernest Gillians
John Glanville
Paul Glanville
Derek Goodrich
David Gray
John Gray
Iain Grayer
Gordon Green
John Green

David Gwilt
Julian Gyngell
Michael Halford
David Hall
Anthony Hamilton
Kenneth Hanson
Timothy Harris
Trevor Harrison
Trevor Hatton
Hugh Hebert
Peter Hecker
Colin Henderson
Giles Heron
George Hetherington
Philip Hinchcliffe
Gerard le Hir
Raymond Hockley
Simon Holding
Michael Holland
John Hollister
John Hollox
David Holmes
Michael Horsley
Francis Hoyland
Nicholas Hudson
Robert Hudson
J Alun Hughes
John Hume
Bryan Humphrey
David Correa Hunt
Timothy Correa Hunt
James Hunter
Martyn Hunter
Herbert Hutchinson
Martin Hyman
Barrie Jameson
Richard Jarrett
David Jeffrey

Hugh Jepson
Martin Johnson
Graeme Johnston
Alan Jones
Glyn Jones
Richard Jones
Robin Jones
Jasper Kay
Jeremy Kaye
Brian King
Michael King
Thomas Klemperer
John Langan
Denis Langford
Alan Lawrance
Christopher Lawson
John Lawson
C F Martin Lawton
Howard Layfield
Peter Leeming
Frank Lees
Christopher Levenson
David Lewis
William Lipscombe
Gordon Littlemore
Brian Livesey
Andrew Long
John McCann
Ernest McDermid
John McFarlane
William McKeown
Desmond McReynolds
Francis Maddison
Albert Maddrell
Keith Manchester
Walter Martin
Lister Mathews
Antony Mauger

David Maxwell
John Melling
John Midgley
Edward Milborrow
Simon Miller
Robert Mills
David Milne
Geoffrey Mitchell
Basil Mogridge
Peter Moll
Richard Morley
David Morrish
Kenneth Moss
Martin Murray
John Myatt
Roy Neal
John Nedderman
Keith Newbitt
Keith Newson
Robert Nickalls
Christopher Noble
John Noon
Robin Norbury
Hugh Norwood
Denis Oakden
Patrick Oakley
Roderick Ogley
Malcolm Page
Bernard Parfrement
Adrian Parsons
Euan Pearson
John Pellow
Edwin Penfold
Raymond Penrose
David Peryer
Richard Pettit
Antony Phillips
Eric Pickup
Peter Pilkington

Christopher Pitt
David Pitt
Michael Pittard
Stephen Platt
John Porritt
Peter Portwood
David Preen
John Prevett
David Pugsley
Graham Putz
Alan Quilley
Arthur Rankine
Brian Ream
Bryan Reed
Colin Reed
Garth Reynolds
Michael Reynolds
Thomas Richardson
Roy Richmond
Ian Ricketts
James Rigby
Alan Roberts
Ernest Roberts
John Roberts
Ian Robins
Ian Robinson
Richard Robinson
David Robson
Peter Robson
Brian Rodmell
William Roff
Andrew Rogers
Frederick Rowley
William Rowley
David Rowntree
Francis Rush
Alan Russell
Martin Samuels
David Saunderson

Jonathan Sayce
Alan Scott
Martin Scott
John Seaman
John Self
John Sennett
Tony Shelley
Graham Shepperd
Doig Simmonds
Donald Simpson
Anthony Derrick Smith
Anthony Godwin Smith
Derek Smith
Douglas Smith
John Brian Smith
John Malcolm Smith
Philip Smith
S Anthony Smith
Timothy Solloway
Colin Sorensen
Christopher Southall
Donald Southall
Hugh Southern
John Southern
Peter Stallabrass
John Stephens
John Stockwell
Robert Stokes
Dennis Stubbs
Joseph Sturge
David Sunderland
Michael Sweet
Arthur Taylor
David G Taylor
David W Taylor
Richard Taylor
James Taylor
John Tempest
Peter Tempest
Philip Tempest

Cyril Thomas
Edwin Thompson
Denis Tomlin
David Tomlinson
Jezdimir Tosic
John Townsend
David Trott
Ian Trott
Keith Tyler
Roy Varnava
Raymond Wadsworth
Gerard Wakeman
David Walker
Keith Wall
Otto Wangermann
Peter Way
Donn Webb
Felix Wedgwood-Oppenheim
Robert Wells
Christopher Whaite
Donald White
Martin Whiteman
John Whitney
David Whitworth
Norman Wilkinson
Brian Williams
Owen Williams
Brian Wills
Anthony Wilson
John Veit Wilson
Richard Wood
Robert Woolley
Donald Wride
Brian Wright
Christopher Wrigley
David Young
Mario Zornoza

TOTAL 354

B: THE ADMINISTRATION OF FAU PWS AND FAUIS

THE FRIENDS AMBULANCE Unit is a charity, governed by a Trust Deed. Control is vested in a committee of management, known until recently as the Council.

During the years 1939-59, the Council, which included the FAU Trustees, delegated responsibility to sub-committees and officers. The war-time Council consisted mainly of older ex-FAU members.

Since the war, younger PWS and IS members have joined the Council and its successor body, the FAU Management Committee. PWS and IS relied heavily on expertise generously offered by some of the busy and distinguished men and women who served on Council during the post-war years.

A copy of the Constitution (as at 1949) and a list of Council members (also as at 1949) is to be found in Appendix IV. The Annual Reports of PWS and IS give updated lists of Council members. The Constitution was amended and updated from time to time, but always in accordance with the Trust Deed.

Council meetings, and all other executive meetings of the Unit, were conducted according to Quaker business methods, so far as was possible in circumstances which were often testing – and which might be most unorthodox. PWS and IS, like the war-time Unit, sometimes worked in close association with larger organisations (such as hospitals and the Red Cross) in which fundamentally different styles of management necessarily prevailed. Members had to be willing to work with (and under) hierarchical authority, *even within the Unit itself*. The management structures of the Unit, including those of the smaller PWS and IS, were finely adapted to balance the requirements of members, the requirements of associated organisations, and the exigencies of the working environment.

Members of the Unit were guided by Standing Orders, and were always subject to the final authority of Council. Staff meetings and Section Meetings (together with occasional

Representative Meetings which ideally consisted of representatives from all sections at home and abroad) helped to ensure that the Unit acted coherently and that its members shouldered a fair measure of responsibility for its work. Members were, by definition, conscientious objectors, and they tended to be individualists. The Unit had to be a thoroughly practical, corporate expression of idealism, so Staff and Section Meetings were an essential, indeed a crucial, part of Unit management.

The management structures which served the war-time Unit so well seem to have worked in PWS and IS, except that Council employed older and more experienced people to act as, for example, full-time General Secretary, Personnel Officer and Finance Officer in PWS and IS. These officers (and the office secretaries) were paid a modest salary, whereas ordinary members were offered only pocket money.

Full membership of the Unit was generally limited to those who shared Quaker views on peace and war (QVPW). To those who came into PWS and IS from abroad and who were either unfamiliar with QVPW or had not been challenged on the issue of conscription to military service, Associate Membership was offered, usually for a period of about six months. All members were required to be Probationary Members for a while at first. Every member had right of direct access to the Chairman of Council, and right of appeal to Council if asked to resign membership.

C: THE FRIENDS AMBULANCE UNIT MEMBERS'
ASSISTANCE FUND

THE MEMBERS' ASSISTANCE Fund was set up in 1941. Its trustees, meeting at Gordon Square on 24 September, took note of a memorandum from the Secretary reporting that a sum provisionally fixed at £646.18.6 was due to be paid to the Fund by the Friends Ambulance Unit and that a further £100 had been promised to the Fund by Mr Paul Cadbury. In those days charities were registered with local government, and the trustees had also to note that London County Council "had taken exception" to a loan of £250 from the FAU Council to the new Fund; it was agreed that this sum should be repaid forthwith. However the Fund was to benefit from generous covenants made even in difficult war-time conditions.

Appropriately enough, since the Members' Assistance Fund (MAF) was taking over from the former Mutual Assistance Fund, one of its first responsibilities was to help members who found they had problems in meeting the cost of life insurance premiums. (Members of the Unit served on a voluntary basis and there was no guarantee of compensation in the event of injury or death in service.) It was later to add to this the payment of personal allowances to members – their "pocket money" – something which continued until the end of 1947, by which time the FAU had been replaced by the Post-War Service. In between, the MAF had also made "post-war training grants" to help members of the war-time FAU to return to their careers, and it was agreed that ex-PWS members could apply for assistance on the same basis. This was later to be extended to ex-members of International Service; in fact such grants were still known as the Post-War Training Fund until 1961, after the closing down of IS, when they became, more appropriately, Educational Grants.

Today the MAF, still a separate registered charity, has lost these regular grant-making activities, but continues to offer limited assistance to former members of FAU, PWS and IS when they need it. There is every hope that it can do so well into the next century.

D: ADVICE TO PROSPECTIVE MEMBERS

THE FOLLOWING OUTLINE was put together in 1952 by the General Secretary to summarise the information most frequently sought by prospective members and other interested in FAU International Service. It was normally sent to applicants together with Application and Medical Examination forms which, when completed, represented the first formal step towards membership.

———

FAUIS – FAU International Service is an activity of the Friends Ambulance Unit, whose members served in Europe, Northern Africa and Asia from 1939 to 1946.

Purpose and Aims – The purpose and aims of the FAUIS are:

- to provide an opportunity for young pacifists, particularly those being registered as conscientious objectors to military service under the provisions of the National Service Acts, to do useful work at home and abroad;

- to encourage young men from overseas to visit this country for the purpose of sharing our life and work;

- to witness our beliefs in service and to encourage international friendships.

Membership – Membership is open to pacifists who agree the Quaker peace testimony. This is broadly interpreted and has not necessarily excluded Atheists. Women pacifists are not currently being accepted, but a list is being kept of those who would consider service in the event of an expansion of the organisation to include opportunities for women members.

Associate Membership – associate membership is open to young, pacifists or not, who are interested to share the life and work of the organisation.

Length of Service – Full members – two years; Associate members (British) – one year; Associate members (other countries) – six months in England (maximum allowed by the Home Office) with possibility of additional service in an overseas section.

Allowances – Allowances for Members and Associates include: Personal Allowance of £2.2.0 per month; Clothing and Toilet Allowance of £1.12.6 per month. Four weeks annual leave with three fares home or alternative allowances. Working clothes or protective clothing. All essential items of maintenance and travel connected with the work are covered by the organisation.

The Work – The work is mostly manual and unskilled, though there is every opportunity to make use of a member's skill in the following types of work: building trades, automobile engineering, secretarial and accountancy, horticulture and agriculture. A full member may ordinarily expect to serve six months in each of the following types of work: forestry, agriculture and related industries or building work, orderly duties in hospitals, overseas relief and reconstruction (mostly building construction, maintenance and repair). In addition members may be called upon to serve as cooks, office workers, house orderlies and in similar capacities essential to the self-dependence of the Unit. Members should be prepared – within reason – to GO ANYWHERE, DO ANYTHING. All war-time members, and particularly those serving in distant parts of the world, accepted this without the protection of the parenthesis. The work programme changes from time to time, but may be expected to remain within the scope of the main headings above.

Policy – Policy is determined by committees and recorded in the Constitution, Standing Orders and Administrative Memoranda, all of which are available to members. All members should read and know the information contained in these documents.

Financial Support – Financial support for the work is derived from subscriptions and from members' earnings. Subscriptions do, to a large extent, determine the volume of overseas work we are free to undertake. All earnings are paid into the General Funds of the organisation. Where need exists we attempt to meet that need in faith that financial support will follow in sufficient measure.

Before closing this Outline, a further word on membership may usefully be said in definition of the picture you may have formed from the preceding information:

Membership involves hard work, possibly for longer hours than regular employment in forestry and agriculture, involves giving, all the time, positively, constructively, physically and spiritually, towards the corporate development and achievement of the Unit, involves discipline, especially in executing Unit work, excludes, by its very nature, being regarded as an easy alternative to military service or as a sacrifice. Please make sure that you *want* to serve as a member of the FAU in preference to any other work which might satisfy a conditional registration as a CO. The following comparisons may help you in your decision:

Forestry, Agriculture, Hospital or other essential work	FAU
A regular income according to national wages decisions	Food, accommodation, travel and other essentials, with small cash allowances
Regular hours and a reasonable certainty of when and where you will be working and what you will be doing	A basis of regular hours plus orderly duties and responsibility to work whenever the need may require – transfers at short notice – no assurance of what you will be doing nor where
Probably, comfortable accommodation	Simple and comfortable accommodation in most sections, but living conditions rough on most overseas sections
Possibly, choice of location of work – e.g. town or country, London or Provinces	Assignment to a section involves living with that section. Much of the work is isolated and conditions are predominantly rural, especially so abroad
Continuing associations with friends and colleagues, and ability to take part in club or society activities	Relatively frequent moves – other members leaving and joining the section – an uncertain opportunity to share activities of musical and dramatic societies or to continue a course of part-time study

Forestry, Agriculture, Hospital or other essential work	FAU
Wages = work done Work done = what others are doing What others are doing = what they have to do or as little as possible or What the Union approves or What wage is worth	The work is not related to wages or other allowances. One should give of one's best whatever the assignment and take as full a share as possible in the corporate life of the Unit, with particular attention to association with foreign members and foreign communities in which we may be working

E: FRIENDS AMBULANCE UNIT COUNCIL AND CONSTITUTION

THE FOLLOWING WERE members of the FAU Council for all or part of the life of FAU Post-War Service and International Service:

Chairman: *Paul S Cadbury

Deputy Chairman: Arnold S Rowntree

Joint Hon. Treasurers: *Basil Priestman FIA

*Joseph A Gillett FCA

Horace G Alexander MA, Margaret Backhouse, John C Bailey BSc, AIM, Sydney D Bailey

*F Ralph Barlow BA, FIHsg, Colin W Bell, Thomas Burns

*Brandon Cadbury BA, Edward Cadbury JP, LLD

Michael H Cadbury, Edgar B Castle MA, E St John Catchpool

*A Tegla Davies MA, Oswald H J Dick, Julian P Fox

*Gerald Gardiner QC, John S Gaskin BSc, Leslie H Gilbert MA, Derek H Goodrich MA, *John H Gray MA, John W Harvey, T Edmund Harvey LLD, J Oliver Holdsworth, *Ronald A Joynes, Eric I Lloyd MA, MB, BCh, FRCS, Leslie B Maxwell OBE, MB, BCh, Patrick H Midgley MB, ChB, William Morley JP, FRGS, Andrew J Morland MD, FRCP, Sir George Newman GBE, KCB, MD, Humphrey Nockolds DSO, MB, BS, FRCS, The Rt. Hon. Philip J Noel-Baker MA, MP, *A E L Parnis BScEcon, John H Robson, *Michael H Rowntree MA (Chairman of the GPC), Hubert Ll Rutter MBE, MD, FRCS, W. Farley Rutter

Eleanor M Sawdon MB, ChB, Herbert G Tanner

Meaburn Tatham OBE, MA, J Michael Vaizey MD, MRCP

*Lewis E Waddilove, Harold Watts, Maurice Webb

Henry Wilson MD, FRCP, J Duncan Wood BA, *John B Wyon MB, MRCP

Eileen Younghusband MBE, JP

* Member of the General Purposes Committee

General Secretary: Ian C Robinson, followed by C Jack Eglon, followed by John R Swindale, followed by Jack Norton

---

The Constitution of Friends Ambulance Unit – International Service, as at 6 May 1949:

1. OBJECT. The Friends Ambulance Unit International Service is a voluntary association of those sharing Quaker views on peace and war. It exists to enable them to give practical expression to their convictions, so far as is within their powers, primarily for the relief of suffering caused by the war and its aftermath, and other socially constructive work.

2. TRUST DEED. The Friends Ambulance Unit International Service is an activity of the Friends Ambulance Unit, itself a charity governed by a Trust Deed dated 20 January 1940.

3. COUNCIL AND COMMITTEES. In a schedule of rules forming part of the Trust Deed, control is vested in a Committee of Management known as The Council. The

Council have delegated control of general policy and administration to a subcommittee known as the General Purposes Committee which meets every three months, and its responsibility for financial policy, bank accounts etc, to its Finance Sub-Committee. The International Service Committee, appointed by the General Purposes Committee on the recommendation of Representative Meeting, had responsibility for detailed policy and administration; it shall meet not less than once every two months.

4. OFFICERS. There shall be two kinds of Officers – Executive Officers and International Service Officers. The General Secretary shall be responsible to the International Service Committee for the day-to-day administration; other Executive Officers shall be responsible through him to the International Service Committee. The General Secretary shall be responsible through the International Service Committee to the Finance Sub-Committee for financial policy and administration, but the Finance Officer shall have right of access to the Finance Sub-Committee. Executive Officers shall be appointed and removed by the Chairman of the General Purposes Committee on the recommendation of the International Service Committee. International Service Officers, such as Section Leaders, shall be appointed and removed by the appropriate Executive Officers, to whom they shall be responsible. In such appointment or removal regard shall be had to the views of the section concerned wherever practicable.

5. REPRESENTATION OF MEMBERS. There shall be a Representative Meeting for the expression of the general will and temper of the International Service. It shall consist of members of the International Service Committee *ex officio*, of any other member asked by the Representative Meeting to serve in an official capacity, and of representatives appointed by home sections, and as far as practicable by every overseas section. A section of one or two members should, wherever possible, combine with another section to send a representative.

Sections of more than twelve members may send two representatives. It shall meet normally every four months and not less than twice a year, make its own rules, appoint its own clerk and other officers, receive reports from the International Service Committee and make recommendations on policy which the International Service Committee is bound to consider.

Representative Meeting may express its lack of confidence in any Executive Officer to the International Service Committee.

In the event of persistent major disagreement between the International Service Committee and the Representative Meeting on a major question of policy or appointment, either party may refer the question to the General Purposes Committee for decision. Representative Meeting may also express its lack of confidence in any member of the International Service Committee to the General Purposes Committee and ask the latter for a decision.

6. MEMBERSHIP. Membership of the International Service shall be of three kinds:

   1) Probationary Membership. Applicants for both full and associate membership (see below) may be admitted to probationary membership, which shall last at least six weeks. No probationary member shall hold office in the International Service.

   2) Associate Membership. This shall be available to those who, subject to having served the full term of probationary membership and having been accepted by the International Service Committee, are not able to serve for more than one year. Associate members shall have equal status to full members.

   3) Full Membership. This shall be limited to those who share Quaker views on peace and war, and who, being prepared to serve for a period which shall not normally be less than two years, and having served the full term of probationary membership, shall be admitted to full membership by the International Service Committee.

All probationary members applying for full membership shall attend a Training Camp. In special cases the International

Service Committee has power to waive this provision. The International Service Committee may waive the condition of probationary membership in the case of ex-members of the Friends Ambulance Unit, and of members admitted for the purpose of becoming Executive Officers.

Members may be asked to resign their membership by the International Service Committee. Any members asked to resign shall have the right of appeal to the General Purposes Committee.

7. DIRECT ACCESS. Any member wishing to make any suggestion or raise any point whatever shall always have right of direct access to the General Secretary, the Chairman of the International Service Committee and the Chairman of the General Purposes Committee.

8. STANDING ORDERS. The International Service Committee shall have the power to issue Standing Orders for the administration and discipline of the International Service, subject to the right of Representative Meeting to review and recommend. As a condition of membership members are required to abide by Standing Orders.

9. AMENDMENT OF THE CONSTITUTION. This Constitution may be amended by the General Purposes Committee on the concurrent recommendations of Representative Meeting and the International Service Committee.

Approved by General Purposes Committee and FAU
International Service Committee
6 May 1949